The Archetypal Hero's Journey in Teaching and Learning

A Study in Jungian Pedagogy

By
Clifford Mayes

Atwood Publishing
Madison, WI

The Archetypal Hero's Journey in Teaching and Learning:
A Study in Jungian Pedagogy

By Clifford Mayes

© 2010, Atwood Publishing, Madison, WI
www.atwoodpublishing.com

All rights reserved.
Printed in the United States of America.

Photos by Mark Smith
Cover design by TLC Graphics, www.tlcgraphics.com

Special thanks to the Friends of Fred Smith for permission to print the cover images.

The Wisconsin Concrete Park is a sculptural environment of over two-hundred embellished concrete sculptures built by Fred Smith, a retired lumberjack and self-taught artist, in Phillips, WI. The site is an historical panorama depicting people, animals, and events from local, regional, and national history, from local lore, and from Smith's expansive imagination. To learn more, visit the website at: www.friendsoffredsmith.org.

Library of Congress Cataloging-in-Publication Data

Mayes, Clifford.
The archetypal hero's journey in teaching and learning : a study in Jungian pedagogy / Clifford Mayes.
p. cm.
Includes bibliographical references and index.
ISBN 978-1-891859-80-9 (pb)
1. Jung, C. G. (Carl Gustav), 1875-1961. 2. Educational psychology. 3. Archetype (Psychology) I. Title.
LB775.J85M385 2010
150.19'54—dc22

2009042252

Contents

Foreword

In Rudolph Otto's foreword to *The Idea of the Holy*, his 1923 landmark work on the role of the numinous in daily life, he explained to his readers that he "ventured to write of that which may be called 'non-rational' or 'supra-rational' in the depths of the divine nature." This moment of "the holy," or the *mysterium tremendum*, takes places when the divine and the natural world intersect, albeit if only briefly. Dr. Clifford Mayes, the leading scholar in what has become known as the archetypal reflectivity movement, demonstrates when that moment takes place in the classroom and instructs teachers in the methods to construct a curriculum where all students are moved beyond the rational and into the realms of what truly connects them to all mankind via depth psychology.

Eschewing the corporate mentality guiding today's curriculum, Dr. Mayes advocates a pedagogy predicated upon the myth of the Hero's (Heroine's) quest, which guides both teachers and students through a series of trials, labors, transformations, and ultimate awakenings. He points out chapter by chapter how the teacher and student form a symbiotic bond while undergoing this alchemical process whereby both are changed, from mere acquaintances at the beginning of the year to true comrades by school's end. Why? Because as Mayes shows, the quest is ultimately about asking and answering the great questions together—questions that transcend the merely secular and speak to the overarching issue of "What am I called do with my life?" Such questions, he persuasively argues, should be at the core of education.

Dr. Carl Gustav Jung, who has heavily influenced Mayes' academic scholarship and personal life, said this about the necessity of the type of curriculum written about in this book:

> One looks back with appreciation to the brilliant teachers, but with gratitude to those who touched our human feelings. The curriculum is so much necessary raw materials,

> but warmth is the vital element for the growing plant and
> for the Soul of the child.

Jung would have been happy to know that Mayes so successfully presents an approach to education aimed at the "soul of the child," as well as that of the teacher.

Mark R. Grandstaff, Ph.D.
Senior Fellow, The James MacGregor Burns Academy of Leadership
The University of Maryland, College Park

Preface

The educational use of the hero myth: beyond corporate education

Near the end of John's gospel, Mary of Magdala, sitting alone at the entrance to Jesus' tomb, fights past her tears to peer inside. In the sepulchral darkness, she makes out two men sitting on either side of the cold empty slab on which Jesus' body had lain. Disconsolate, she does not recognize them as heavenly messengers. When they ask her why she is weeping, she replies, "They have taken my Lord away, and I do not know where they have laid him." John then goes on to report:

> With these words she turned round and saw Jesus standing there, but did not recognize him. Jesus said to her, "Why are you weeping? Who is it you are looking for?" Thinking it was the gardener, she said, "If it is you, Sir, who removed him, tell me where you have laid him, and I will take him away." Jesus said, "Mary!" She turned to him and said, "Rabbuni!" (which is Hebrew for "My Master"). (*NEB*. John 20: 14–16)

It has always seemed to me that almost as remarkable as the account of the resurrection itself is Mary's response to Jesus. She calls him "Rabbuni." This word, the highest honorific title in Hebrew, derives from "Rabbi"—or "Teacher." As in the Semitic languages generally, there is no greater compliment or sign of devotion than to call someone "my teacher."

So here we have Mary realizing that she is speaking to a resurrected being, and what are the first words out of her mouth? She calls him "Master and Teacher." This masterful teacher is humbly dressed. He could even be mistaken for a gardener. Mary addresses him reverentially, but he seems to deflect this somewhat by turning the focus back onto her—his student. Or rather, he affirms *his* identity by establishing *her* identity, by uttering *her* name, "Mary!" Mary as a student experiences new life through revived dialogue with her teacher. Indeed, Jesus's fundamental identity as a teacher, and the parables that he continually deploys in his discourses, suggest the tight interweaving of spiritual growth and pedagogical conversation in John's gospel.

Now, I am not trying to suggest here that teachers should see themselves as messiahs and their students as worshipers. Indeed, when teachers do see things this way, it is usually a prelude to all sorts of intellectual, moral, and political mischief. Nor is it my intention in this book to provide a "theology of teaching." Instead, I am interested here in the scene between Jesus and Mary Magdala because of its pedagogical significance in pointing to the fundamentally sacred nature of the teacher–student relationship. It is to examine and celebrate the sanctity of the teacher–student relationship that I have written this book.

I am aware that some will accuse me of putting too fine a point upon pedagogical issues to characterize the educative relationship in spiritual terms. But consider. We are involved in crucially important acts of teaching and learning throughout our lives. In anything of any significance that we say or do, hope or fear, affirm or deny, we are manifesting to the world what we have learned (or failed to learn) from others—simultaneously providing a model for others to use or reject in their own ongoing existential education. This is true from cradle to grave. The infant and mother negotiate with and "teach" each other about the delicate protocols and deeper meanings of nursing in the quiet intimacy of the feeding hour. And at the other end of the life-cycle, we know how to die well because we have observed others (usually loved ones) as they passed through the experience with integrity, humor, and even hope.

I believe that a culture's views and practices regarding something so fundamental to the human experience as teaching and learning will naturally tell us a great deal about that culture itself. What counts as "important knowledge," and the way in which that knowledge is supposed to be constructed and conveyed, especially to its young people, mirrors the culture's values. This is why it is of more than just specialized, passing interest that in colleges of education across the United States today—and, indeed, in a growing number of educational sites generally in the post-industrial Western world—education is increasingly being reduced to a quasi-science, a "norm-referenced" and "statistically validated" body of impersonal, decontextualized techniques and tools whose basic purpose is to get students to score well on standardized tests. Where a culture's views and practices regarding education are becoming so reductive, we have reason to fear that the culture in general is in danger of becoming diminished.

There is a history to the merely "functional" approach to teaching and learning that is increasingly coming to govern American education, and it began in schools and colleges of education around the turn of the twentieth century.

The mechanistic view of teachers and students—indeed, human beings in general—was announced in the early 1900s by such social "scientists" as Edward Thorndike—the father of psychometrics and famous professor of education at Columbia University's Teachers College—in his terse and terrible pronouncement that intelligence not only could, but *must* be scientifically defined, categorized, and quantified. For, "whatever exists, exists in some amount and can be measured," he declaimed. This was a view that went down well with an American society that was beginning to really flex its military and industrial muscles in historically unique and internationally consequential ways. The problem with Thorndike's mathematical approach to life in its entirety ("whatever exists") is that although it works well in designing a can opener, building a bridge, or predicting the trajectory of a missile—it is absurdly inadequate in grasping those immeasurably complex and delicate interactions that go on (physically, emotionally, cognitively, culturally, and ethically) between a teacher and a student in the classroom. Approaching teaching and learning in such simplistic, mechanistic terms makes about as much sense as trying to perform neurosurgery wearing boxing gloves.

Nevertheless, throughout the first half of the twentieth century the Thorndikian educational agenda increasingly won the day, overshadowing what the Progressive movement had to offer in the psychologically dynamic pedagogies of Caroline Pratt and Caroline Zachry, the democratically empowering pedagogies of John Dewey and George Counts, and the academically rich pedagogies of Boyd Bode and William Bagley. That this should have been the case was hardly surprising in a country where, as one of its presidents had recently informed the public, "The business of America is business."

Thorndike's "scientistic" views of education foreshadowed the appearance in 1956 of that chilling manifesto of standardized instruction and assessment—B. F. Skinner's *The Technology of Teaching*. In this stingy and sterile view of teaching and learning, the classroom is seen as a factory, the teacher a foreman, and the students, assembly-line workers. The goal is to use principles of scientific management in order to "maximize educational outputs" (a phrase that is still much in vogue in educational policy and scholarship), as measured by student performance on standardized tests.

These tests are touted as ways of measuring "knowledge," but anyone who has ever taken a standardized test knows that they do no such thing. In point of fact, the test is simply meant to quantify how well a student can "master" (that is to say, memorize) unrelated bits of information, (which the student will promptly forget as soon as the test is over), in areas that have themselves been dissociated from each other (for "ease and efficiency of assessment"). In this manner, schooling becomes, as Joel Spring (1976) has so felicitously put it, a "sorting machine"—a way (indeed, *the* way) of institutionally determining which students will play what roles as "worker–citizens" in our brave new corporate society—that real–life dystopia that is now controlled by an increasingly select, powerful, and covert socioeconomic elite—what Paul Simon has portrayed in one of his songs as "a loose affiliation of millionaires and billionaires"; what Friedman (2000) calls "the electronic herd" of venture–capitalists, armed with laptops and ceaselessly in search of fresh politico-economic prey to dominate and devour; and what Peter Dale Scott (2007) has brilliantly identified as the "deep political system" of covert military–fiscal interests that increasingly control the United States today.

Slyly mouthing platitudes about "democracy" and "free enterprise" in the service of "the nation," the new masters' appetites and strategies are actually transnational, their reach global, their manipulation of the media subtle, even sexy. Their armies are multinational conglomerates, especially protective geopolitically of areas containing precious, scarce resources. Their high-tech means of surveillance and influence are finely attuned to even the slightest economic and political tremor anywhere, anytime, on the new electronically interconnected planet, for it is in this way that old markets can be abandoned at a profit and new ones can be predicted (or created) and controlled at the push of a button on a laptop computer.

In other words, Huxley's and Orwell's prophecies have come to pass (or will very soon do so), and the pedagogical consequences are everywhere to be seen. Education—that sacred enterprise of wisely and lovingly developing every aspect of a person's being, in what my faith-tradition calls the individual's journey of "eternal progression" —is being taken captive and turned into a colossal corporate program of diminishing, even eradicating, the student's full humanity. When students can not, or will not, submit to this psychological and spiritual violence, they are diagnosed as having medical problems that require pharmaceutical treatments in the form of a new generation of psychotropic drugs that simultaneously numb students deeper sensibilities and sharpen their "focus" on the sterile tasks at hand.

Unfortunately, it is no exaggeration to say that American education—whether at the elementary, secondary, or tertiary levels—is increasingly operating under the long shadow of the military-fiscal complex. We would do well to recall the warning given in 1988 by the premier American educational historian of the twentieth century, Lawrence Cremin. Cremin, echoing the alarm that President Eisenhower expressed in his farewell speech in 1961 at the expansion of the military-industrial complex, declared that as the twentieth century drew to a close and the new one began, the primary educational problem facing the United States would be the cancerous growth of the military-fiscal-*educational* complex.

This book represents an attempt to resist the incursion of the military-fiscal complex into education by envisioning and celebrating teaching and learning in terms that are psychosocially, ethically, and spiritually ennobling both for teachers and students. I intend to do this by examining teaching and learning from a mythic point of view, using the archetypal Hero's Journey as my frame of reference. Drawing on Joseph Campbell's (1949) classic study of the archetypal Hero's Journey in search of individual and social redemption, *The Hero with a Thousand Faces*, my goal is to offer a psychospiritually rich, politically valid, and pedagogically useful way of respectfully approaching and carefully guarding the mysteries of education.

TEACHING, LEARNING, AND THE HERO'S JOURNEY

Looking at teaching and learning as an archetypal Hero's Journey is a good way of talking about education in its psychological and spiritual depths because the Hero's Journey is fundamentally an educative one. This is so because the Hero's Journey is not ultimately just a charming and action-packed story about how a hero enters a forest or desert of trials and tribulations, meets with helpers and enemies, slays a monster, finds a mate, returns home as a conquering hero to his or her[1] village-home, or any of the other events that the hero passes through. Ultimately, the Hero's Journey is a symbol. What it symbolizes is the emotional, intellectual, and spiritual growth of the individual as he or she goes beyond the narrow confines of family and immediate environment in order to seek, find, and ultimately act on a new vision of self, society, world, and cosmos.

In other words, the Hero's Journey is about nothing less than asking and answering the big questions: Where did I come from? Is there a purpose for my being here? What should I do and what should I not do in order to not only endure this earthly experience but to emerge from it as the most intelligent, insightful, humane, and efficacious person that I am capable of being? What is wisdom and what is love, and how can I be as wise and loving as possible in the various kinds of relationships with others in my life that, ultimately, *are* my life? And finally, what, if anything, lies beyond the grave for me and for my fellow human beings? Is there hope that we may continue to live and love together beyond this life, and, if so, what is the best way to carry on this life in light of that hope? These are the questions that are the core of the Hero's Journey. They should also be at the core of education. Examining the Hero's Journey will therefore tell us a very great deal about the educational journey—its origins, processes, and goals—in terms that go beyond the standard rubrics of educational discourse.

The hero's myth begins with a person, usually a young man or woman, receiving some form of a "call"—often announced in a dream, delivered by a mystical animal, or issued as a challenge from a high-ranking personage. The call requires the hero to leave the simple pleasures, easy routines, and comfortable security of home, clan, and village in order to go alone into an "arena" of trials and tribulations. This arena is typically a dense forest, enormous desert, vast plain, rugged mountain, daunting ocean, or some other frightening natural setting. The youth must decide whether or not to accept this call to adventure. If the potential hero refuses the call, he or she is usually beset by a host of unhappy occurrences, ranging from minor inconveniences to deathly threats. These will continue until the youth agrees to heed the call and embark upon the journey.

But the hero—although basically on a solitary quest—is not left utterly alone in his or her momentous business. Upon crossing the threshold into the forest or desert, ocean or plain, the hero typically meets a Wise Old Man or Wise Old Woman[2] who provides the hero with powerful potions, charming amulets, signs and tokens, and sage advice that will serve the hero often and well throughout his or her passage down the Road of Trials.

One of the most important episodes in this journey is when the hero happens upon and enters a secret cave, deserted mansion, or some other large, dark enclosure suggestive of the womb. Upon emerging from this structure, the hero engages in his or her most difficult battle, often with a monster, knight, or demon. If he or she prevails, a great reward is in store. Often the reward is in the form of an enchanted sword or priceless gem that endows the privileged hero with almost divine authority and power.

The decision now facing the hero is the obverse of the one with which the story began. For the hero must now decide whether or not to *leave* the mystical realm—in which so much has been suffered, learned, and won—in order to *return* to his or her native land, where the greatly empowered hero can restore and enrich the homeland. If the hero does not do this, then he or she will remain in the mystical realm, living in a cottage in happy marital seclusion or as a hermit who will serve as a Wise Old Man or Wise Old Woman with special insight and power to proffer the next generation of heroes who will cross the threshold, seeking adventure and transformation.

In what follows, we look at the educational significance of each of these archetypal persons and events.

NOTES

1. I use the term "hero" to refer to both men and women. Regarding pronoun usage, I either use he/she constructions or alternate between male and female pronouns—as rhetorical necessity warrants. In all cases, I aim at gender-fairness in both what is written and how it is written.

2. Throughout this study, I capitalize the names of archetypal characters. In Chapter 2 I define what an archetypal character is.

CHAPTER 1

Psychodynamic Essentials

Personal and transpersonal psychology

In order to understand and use the power of the psychospiritually rich Hero's Journey in one's teaching, it is necessary to discuss some of the basic elements of depth psychology, focusing upon neo-Freudian theory. Equally important is a grasp of some of the basic elements of *transpersonal* psychology.[1] For the reader who may not be familiar with transpersonal psychology, a few introductory words are in order.

As its name suggests, *trans*-personal psychology goes beyond (but never ignores) the personal, "biographical" experiences and issues that constitute the individual's unique psyche. Transpersonal psychology ventures into the most profound of inner realms where the individual's psyche begins, in a sense, to go beyond itself—past ego consciousness, even past the personal subconscious—into a region that, common to all human beings in all places and eras, partakes of the transcendent and timeless. This realm, connecting us at the most fundamental levels of our being to each other and the Divine, is called "the collective unconscious" (Jung 1968a).

The collective unconscious speaks to us most clearly in its own natural, symbolic language of "myth"—the images, motifs, and sacred stories that are the foundation of psyche and culture (Lévi-Strauss 1987). Please note that I use the term "myth" throughout this study to mean any story that a group of people tells and believes in and that is culturally foundational. Whether or not the story is "true" (in the simple, historical sense of having actually happened, or having happened exactly as reported) does not concern me here. I am neutral in this study as to a myth's historical veracity. I consider a myth *true* if it provides a group of people with social, ethical, and spiritual rootedness and guidance.

The Hero's Journey is one of the most important of these myths emanating from the collective unconscious. It is to be found throughout history and in every society. Naturally, the characters and settings of myths will vary from era to era, and from society to society, but the essence of the myth—its structure and meaning—will more or less follow the patterns and purposes explained above. Approaching teaching and learning in the context of this myth's spiritual power will allow us to approach the educational enterprise in spiritual terms.

A great advantage of using the Hero myth in examining education is that it approaches spirituality in teaching and learning without privileging any particular religious view. Indeed, it need not refer to religion, as such, at all. As Abraham Maslow, the father of transpersonal psychology, wrote, transpersonal psychology offers an important way for people in the more "developed" Western societies (many of whom now no longer really believe in the doctrines of any organized religion) a way to access "the naturalistically transcendent, spiritual, and axiological" within themselves. Maslow thus called transpersonal psychology "religion with a little 'r'," because it does not require or necessarily lead to formal religious commitments (Maslow 1968, vi). All it asks is that the individual look beyond mere ego and personal identity in order to search for the Divine in himself or herself. This is crucially important, Maslow said, because, "without the transpersonal, we get sick, violent, and nihilistic, or else hopeless and apathetic," due to a feeling of disconnection from the Divine, which is our primary source and ultimate goal as human beings (1968, vi).

In this book, I focus upon the transpersonal psychology of C. G. Jung and its development by first-, second-, and third-generation neo-Jungians, for Jungian psychology is the most powerful of all the transpersonal psychologies—and certainly the one best suited to approaching the mystery of the Hero's myth.

Freud's Sexual Hypothesis—and Beyond

Freudian psychology is often seen as a revolving entirely around sexual issues. Certainly, there is a heavy emphasis on sexuality in Freud's writings. However, as early as 1914, Freud had entertained the possibility that there were "various points in favor of the hypothesis of a primordial differentiation between sexual instincts and other instincts, ego instincts" (1957 [1914], 106). In other words, sex was important, even central, to psychological functioning, according to

Freud; however, the birth and growth of the ego was also important and would come to figure more and more prominently in his picture of the psyche. Thus, as Freud's thinking evolved, he spent an increasing amount of time studying the origin, structure, and evolution of the ego, which he saw as a dynamic, shifting field of memories, perspectives, tendencies, and capacities that we call "conscious awareness." This germinal interest in the ego would blossom in the second half of the twentieth century into what is called "ego psychology" and "self psychology" in the work of later psychoanalytically-oriented theorists and practitioners such as Heinz Kohut, D. W. Winnicott, and W. R. D. Fairbairn, each of whom are examined below.

In the last phase of his writing and practice, Freud would expand the notion of *libido*, which he had previously seen as merely sexual energy, calling it *Eros* and depicting it as a sort of generalized life-instinct (still primarily involved with sexuality, but probably not quite completely reducible to it) which was constantly doing battle with a death-instinct that he called *Thanatos*—or the desire of every creature to return to a state of eternal rest in the primal womb of being. In this war, death must inevitably triumph. "The goal of all life is death," declared Freud in *Beyond the Pleasure Principle*, for "the inanimate was there before the animate" (1957 [1923], 160).

Transference and Counter-Transference

One of Freud's most important insights regards what he called "the transference," which figures prominently in the pages that follow.

Greenson has summarized the classical view of the transference as "the experiencing of feelings, drives, attitudes, fantasies, and defenses toward a person in the present which are inappropriate to that person and are a repetition, a displacement of reactions originating in regard to significant persons of early childhood" (1990, 151). In other words, the transference is, as Freud put it, "a new edition" of an old problem (1970 [1915-1917], 462)—a *repetition compulsion* in which the patient projects images and issues from his early childhood onto the psychotherapist, usually involving the parents or other immediate caregivers.

The goal of therapy—and the tricky task of the therapist—is to work with the patient's transferences in a way that will finally resolve the issue that underlies the transference, thereby eliminating the need for adult repetition of the original problem. The analyst must be able to "contain" the *transference neurosis*—that is, the *projections* of the patient onto him or her—in such a way that the patient can play the old issues out again, but this time begin to deal with them in the consulting room. In a sense, therefore, the relationship between the analyst and patient is more important to a cure than any particular theoretical or technical orientations on the part of the therapist. This is why Freud believed that "the outcome in this struggle [to overcome a psychological problem] is not decided by [the patient's] intellectual insight—it is neither strong enough nor free enough to accomplish such a thing—but solely by his relationship with the physician" (Freud 1970 [1915–1917], 453).[2]

Freud spoke of the transference as being either *syntonic* or *dystonic*—that is, either positive or negative. "We must make up our minds to distinguish a 'positive' transference from a 'negative' one, the transference of affectionate feelings from that of hostile ones, and to treat the two sorts of transference to the doctor separately" (1990, 32). The perils and potentials of transference in psychoanalysis are so central to the whole endeavor that Henderson (1967) has called the transference the *pièce de résistance* of psychoanalysis. Indeed, Freud himself is reported to have heartily approved of the characterization of the transference as "the alpha and omega" of therapy (Jung and Jaffé 1965).

The transference is not a one-way street. Just as the patient projects psychic issues onto the analyst, so the analyst may (and perhaps inevitably does) project his psychic issues back onto the patient. This is known as *the counter-transference*, and it can be especially powerful if the patient is projecting psychic energy onto the analyst that touches one of the analyst's own psychic wounds. "If the analyst is not aware of his or her own shadow response, real harm can be done" as the analyst projects his or her issues back onto the unsuspecting and vulnerable patient (Woodman 1995, 54).

For instance, let us say that a female patient projects her need to be protected by a father-figure onto her analyst. Let us further assume that the analyst had a very dependent mother whom he felt it was his duty to protect from the world. If he has not already resolved this issue, such an analyst, unconsciously driven by the false notion that his job in life is to save "damsels in distress," may be especially prone to fall prey to his client's subconscious cries for protection by a father-figure. This could undermine the whole purpose of the therapy, which would be to help the woman gain greater independence in life, not to reinforce her patterns of dependency. To make matters even more complex, it sometimes happens that the analyst's counter-transference happens independently of anything the patient has done or any issues the patient has. The analyst in our example may project his need to save females onto his patient even though she has not sent any signals at all that she needs saving by a father-figure. It was not until the late 1940s, however, close to the time of Freud's death, that the psychoanalytic movement began to show a widespread interest in the counter-transference and its therapeutic possibilities.[3]

Neo-Freudian Theorists

In this section, the focus is on three of the most important psychoanalytic theorists who followed Freud. Their thoughts have proven to be especially important in educational theory.[4] Although the three psychoanalytic theorists differ in important ways, they, along with many other neo-Freudians, share some basic reservations about and revisions to classical psychoanalytic theory.

First, they question Freud's "hydraulic" or "plumbing" model of the psyche, with its vision of the subconscious as unrelenting, blind instincts, always threatening, like toxic gasses in a cramped container, to explode and wound the fragile ego in the form of a neurotic symptom, or even shatter the ego in a psychotic break. Even those few recent theorists who still do hold to a model of psyche that relies upon the notion of instinct (most neo-Freudians now see in that model an outdated metaphor of the human organism from nineteenth century biology) picture those instincts as *including, but not limited to, sexual ones.*

Second, the basic psychological motivation is seen as being the desire to enter into relationship with a significant other or others, and to do so in such a way as to establish and maintain a sense of personal identity and empowerment. Sex is certainly a powerful motivator; but according to the neo-Freudians whom we examine here, it is the need for relationship that is primary; sex is secondary. Indeed, the urgency of the sexual drive may largely be due to the fact that it is a particularly intense form of relationship. Third, certain neo-Freudians see *psychological health* not as the containment of primordial impulses, but as the pursuit of ethically and even spiritually significant purposes that provide a person with moral direction, spiritual meaning, and, in general, personal fulfillment in his or her life (Meissner 1984; Rizzuto 1979; Schafer 1980).

Heinz Kohut

Heinz Kohut is the father of "self-psychology," which views the striving for a stable and holistic sense of self as the primary psychodynamic impulse. Sexual issues will certainly come into play in defining and maintaining a self, as will many other issues, but they will all be oriented to the life-goal of self-definition and self-maintenance (Eagle 1993, 40)—what Kohut called a state of ***healthy narcissism***. The person who does not have such a relatively stable and unified sense of self suffers from a ***narcissistic wound*** (Kohut 1978). The foundations of a person's sense of self reside in his earliest relationships with primary caregivers—or *selfobjects*, so called because they are the objects of the infant's earliest attention and affection through whom the infant learns about the world and itself (Kohut 1978). It is important to remember that the selfobject is not, in the final analysis, actually the other person or thing that is helping an individual define himself but is the *image* of that person or thing that the infant (and later the adult) has internalized—or, in psychoanalytic parlance, has *introjected*.

Typically, the infant's central selfobject is its mother. The infant's psyche is so dramatically shaped by its interaction with its mother because it is symbiotically fused with her at this primal stage. Indeed, in the infant's earliest view, the mother is indistinguishable from itself, according to many psychoanalytic theorists.[5] If the mother's interaction with the infant communicates love and acceptance, the infant begins to assume that it is loveable and accepted and that the world is essentially dependable and beneficent. The infant comes to see itself as a good, stable, and integrated being. In short, the child's *primary narcissism* (Kohut 1978, 430) finds confirmation and gratification in its union with the loving mother, and it does so in two basic ways.

The first is in *the mirroring transference,* which consists in the infant seeing itself through the mirror of its mother's responses to it. The second is in *the idealizing transference,* in which the infant, enshrining the mother as not only the apex of reality but indeed as reality itself, finds its own ideals in its merger with this godly personage. The "idealized parental imago … is gazed at in awe, admired, looked up to, and [is that] which one wants to become" (Kohut 1978, 430). The idealizing transference is the root of the child's ability to define, have, and maintain values (Eagle 1993, 54).

The opposite of this kind of value-instilling mother is the one who communicates to the infant, in how she interacts with it, that she is unhappy that it has come into the world, unduly anxious about it, or repelled by it. This lays the foundation for a variety of psychic disorders in the developing infant and eventually in the adult—especially *the narcissistic personality disorders*. For, what the infant sees in the "mirror" of the mother is its own undesirability, inadequacy, and lack of unity. The infant thereby learns as well—in a colossal failure of the idealizing transference—that the world is neither welcome nor welcoming, but is rather rejecting, cold, dangerous, and confusing, and that it is a place that is either valueless or that has values that are unattainable or irrelevant. The narcissistic personality disorders are pathological attempts to experience the primary mirroring and idealizing that the person as an infant never experienced—or never experienced sufficiently (Kohut 1978, 440, 478). These pathological manifestations are forms of *secondary narcissism*. Healthy human development thus originates in primary narcissism and concludes in healthy narcissism. When primary narcissistic needs are not met, the many dysfunctions of secondary narcissism result.

In his later work especially, Kohut focuses on the relationship between healthy narcissism and productivity. He explores "the ways by which a number of complex and autonomous achievements of the mature personality [are] derived from transformations of narcissism —i.e., created by the ego's capacity to tame narcissistic cathexes and to employ them for its highest aims" (1978, 460). Humor, empathy, wisdom, and creativity are fruits of the positive transformation of primary narcissism into mature narcissism.

D. W. Winnicott

From the extraordinarily rich body of work of the British child psychotherapist D. W. Winnicott, we look at three concepts which have significant educational implications: *holding environments*, *good-enough mothering*, and *transitional objects*.

Like Kohut, Winnicott sees the roots of psychic health or illness in the infant's relationship with its mother. Ideally, the mother will provide a good *holding environment* for the infant. This may actually involve the physical act of lovingly holding the infant. Yet even when it does not, it does entail the mother providing the child with a physical and emotional context that is appropriate to its needs and beneficial to its growth—an environment, in short, that *holds* the child so that the child can mature in safety:

> A wide extension of "holding" allows this one term to describe all that a mother does in the physical care of her baby, even including putting the baby down when a moment has come for the impersonal experience of being held by suitable non-human materials. In giving consideration to these matters, it is necessary to postulate a state of the mother who is (temporarily) identified with her baby so that she knows without thinking about it more or less what

> the baby needs. She does this, in health, without losing her own identity. (Winnicott 1988, 259)

Note Winnicott's insistence that the mother should provide not only adequate holding for the child, but also that she should do so "without losing her own identity." Good mothering does not mean *perfect* mothering, in which the mother must always be available to the infant, meeting its every need almost before it arises. A so-called "perfect" mother would have to forego her own identity, needs, and boundaries. Such *perfect* treatment of the infant, far from actually *being* perfect, is flawed, for it does not allow the infant to experience those moments of opposition that are necessary for it to experience—in healthy and monitored doses, of course—so that it can begin to mature. A mother who psychically fuses with her infant to such an extent that she completely forfeits her own healthy sense of boundaries will present to the infant an unhealthy example of what relationship means. On the other hand, *good-enough mothering* prevents burn-out in the mother by providing for her own identity and even occasional mistakes. "Good-enough mothering gives opportunity for the steady development of personal processes in the baby" (Winnicott 1988, 456)—processes that will feed positively upon the mother's realistic humanity and not her neurotic perfectionism. Needless to say, such mothering is still fundamentally loving, careful, and adequate to the infant's physical and psychic development. Good-enough mothering provides for the mother's increasing separateness from the child as it begins to mature—a process best embodied and symbolized in weaning. With increasing separation, the infant, and then the older child, comes to sense both physically and emotionally the existentially necessary lesson that there is a grand divide between the world of Me and Not-Me—the Not-Me world first being experienced by the child as the withdrawing and sometimes even absent mother.

To negotiate the space between the world of Me and Not-Me, the infant will come to rely upon a *transitional object.* To take a prime example: the infant's own thumb, which replaces the mother's breast when the infant wishes to nurse but the mother is not available for feeding, is the first transitional object. The thumb, through a basic exercising of the infant's still primitive imagination, comes to replace the absent breast. The thumb is no longer just a thumb to the infant, although the child does not mistake it for a breast either; rather, the thumb becomes a transitional object—a psychologically living symbol whose significance and power lie in the fact that the child's imagination invests it with the power to satisfy at least some of its needs. In the same way, a favorite blanket becomes the child's substitute for the mother when she is away. Through creative fantasy, the child turns the blanket into a transitional object that is now not just a blanket or a mother but a "poetic" fusion of both.

> The thumb stands for an external or NOT-ME object, is symbolical of it, as we would say. The external object being sufficiently available, it can be used as substitute. This transition is itself allowed to take place slowly and gradually, in the infant's own time. Transitional objects [such as pieces of cloth, dolls, teddy-bears, toys, or what have you] are provided or are adopted which (when the infant is resting from the arduous process of sorting out the world and the self) are cuddled or pushed away without being classified as thumb or breast symbols. (Winnicott 1988, 436)

As the child develops, it chooses more complex transitional objects to symbolically express and deal with the existential gap between its inner and outer realities. In a sense, therefore, all of our philosophical and artistic products, our concepts and images, are highly evolved transitional objects through which we express our fundamental existential need to interpret and interact with external reality. The transitional space is the place, and the transitional object is the thing, where the interior world of "I" and the exterior world of "Other" can come into creative contact. Winnicott even goes so far as to suggest that culture is a collective transitional social object in which a group of people experience and express their shared experience of reality.

W. R. D. Fairbairn

Fairbairn's basic idea is that "libido is not pleasure-seeking, but object-seeking" (Eagle 1993, 75). It is not primal drives that energize the psyche, but the need to enter into human relationship. "It must always be borne in mind . . . that it is not the libidinal attitude which determines the object-relationship, but the object-relationship which determines the libidinal attitude" (Fairbairn 1992, 34).

What is most interesting about this important theorist for our purposes as educationists, however, is Fairbairn's insistence that over-intellectualization can represent "a general tendency on the part of individuals with a schizoid component to heap up their values in an inner world"—attempting thereby to avoid and create a substitute for actual relationships with other people in the real world of emotional give-and-take (Fairbairn 1992, 8). Fairbairn is here talking about individuals who would almost always rather be buried in a book or sequestered in a lonely lab, rather than be with other people. "This high libidinization of the thought process," wrote Fairbairn, is characteristic of people who "are often more inclined to develop intellectual systems of an elaborate kind than to develop emotional relations with others on a human basis"; indeed, such individuals are inclined "to make libidinal objects of the systems which they have created" in lieu of the pleasure of human contact (Fairbairn 1992, 21). Intellectualization, "a very characteristic schizoid feature," can thus be misused as an:

> extremely powerful defense technique [which often operates] as a very formidable resistance in psychoanalytical therapy. Intellectualization implies an overvaluation of the thought-processes; and this overvaluation of thought is related to the difficulty which the individual with a schizoid tendency experiences with making emotional contacts with other people. (Fairbairn 1992, 20)

Beyond Personal Psychodynamics: Transpersonal Psychospirituality

Transpersonal psychology acknowledges the necessity of dealing with the psyche at the personal level of Freudian and neo-Freudian theory, but it also insists on the need to move beyond that realm into a region in which psyche begins to transcend its family-of-origin issues and approach the universal, timeless realm of Spirit. Only by attending to both personal and transpersonal aspects of the psyche is it possible to address the complete spectrum of human motivations, problems, and potentials—from the most primal to the most transcendent, from sex with a mate to communion with Divinity. In this book we focus on Jungian psychology because it is was the first, and is still the best, of the many transpersonal psychologies that have emerged over the last four decades.

Jung, once Freud's premier disciple, ultimately broke with Freud around 1913. Jung increasingly believed that Freud's sexual hypothesis—although "a faithful picture of real facts that force themselves upon our observation"—was far from the whole story about how the psyche works. Jung argued that reducing the many mysterious aspects of psyche to "nothing but" one animalistic drive or other, or even an assemblage of them, was simplistic, counter-intuitive, and morally belittling to the human being as a complex moral and spiritual agent (1966, par. 68).

Jung's objections were not merely academic. They were also medical. It became more and more evident to Jung in both his clinical practice and scientific investigations that the appetites for sex and power are themselves ultimately just "fragments" that emerge from an even deeper realm of psychic functioning. This realm represents the ancient, primary, and transcendent center of the human psyche. This psychic center, Jung believed, was the very place where the human psyche came into closest contact with Divinity itself—where the human mind and the Divine Mind intersected (Jung 1953, par. 199). At the very nucleus of psyche, then, is not the appetite for sex or the drive for power (as important as those things may be). Rather, it is the longing for communion with the Divine that lies at the very center of one's being and powers psychic functioning. Discovery of one's innermost "Self" (which Jungians capitalize in order to distinguish it from the much more superficial, ego-centered "self" of daily consciousness) is tantamount to communion with God, for God dwells in our innermost Self and speaks to us from there.

This was Jung's psychological interpretation of St. Paul's proclamation: "The life I now live is not my life, but the life which Christ lives in me" (*NEB*. Galatians 2: 20). Paul was indicating that he had moved beyond the ordinary realm of mere ego-consciousness and had accessed his higher Self in union with God. This merger is the primary goal of most transpersonal psychology, which sees psychological health as being impossible if a person does not have some fundamental sense of connection with the Spirit (however he or she uniquely understands and experiences Spirit).

However, Jung and the transpersonalists would never claim that ego-consciousness is unimportant. Quite to the contrary. To lose ego-consciousness is to lose touch with day-to-day reality, and the word for that is psychosis—the last thing that Jung, or any transpersonal psychotherapist, would want to happen! Indeed, Jung was himself a very pragmatic Swiss gentleman, a family man, and a rather conservative fellow, who was proud of being a physician-captain in the Swiss militia. He had grown up and chose as an adult to live in the rugged countryside, where he saw patients on a daily basis and spent most of his extra hours cooking, gardening, painting, and working in stone. He understood full well that ego-consciousness is absolutely essential to psychological health.

His point was simply that if an individual is to live an experientially rich and ethically authentic life, then that person's ego-consciousness should always be attentive to the symbols, intuitions, and inspirations that come from his or her core, the Self. The Self is the inner temple where the Divine descends to address a particular person in the most intensely personal ways. This conversation between an individual and the Divine neither relies upon nor prohibits commitment to a specific religious dogma. This accords with common sense, for we all know people who have no particular religious affiliation but seem to be in touch with eternal realities and are humane in their actions towards others. We also all know people who, like the man in the story, prays on his knees every Sunday—and then preys on his neighbors the other days of the week!

Healthy psychological functioning consists, therefore, in establishing a connection (or an "axis" as Jungian psychologists call it) between the ego and the Self—between the everyday world of practical consciousness and the interior world of spiritual intuition (Edinger 1973). This ego-Self axis empowers one to live a life that is both practical and transcendent. Indeed, the growth of this ego-Self axis is what Jung meant by "individuation," which he saw as the highest goal of not only therapy but of life itself.

Jung's challenge as a psychiatrist was to find theoretical constructs and useful terms that would allow him as a psychotherapist to understand and work with this realm where psyche becomes spirit, where ego meets Self, and where Self encounters its God—a region that is both intensely personal and transcendentally universal. Are there terms, concepts, or models that can be deployed to help the therapist approach this mystery and tap its healing power? Jung would ultimately find an answer to these questions in his idea of "the archetypes" and "the collective unconscious."

THE ARCHETYPES AND THE COLLECTIVE UNCONSCIOUS

Jung was adept in various ancient languages and widely read in ancient literature and myth. This linguistic and literary prowess came to play an important role from early on in his career as a psychiatrist. As an intern psychiatrist in the Berghölzi Clinic in Zurich, he had begun to note—in both his daily rounds and nightly readings—uncanny and seemingly inexplicable correspondences between the dreams that his patients presented, on one hand, and the patterns, plots, and personages of many ancient myths, on the other hand. Seeing so many of these impressive parallels between a patient's inner life and various cultures' sacred stories (which his patients had generally never heard or read before), Jung suspected that they might provide an entrée into that inner personal realm where the individual psyche meets the ancient, even eternal, realm of spirit.

At any rate, one thing was becoming clear to Jung in his clinical experience—and it was that sexual energy is not the bedrock of psychic functioning. Rather, at the nucleus of human consciousness is a web of "energies"—some sexual, but mostly not—which are innate, universal, and ultimately Spirit-oriented. These energies manifest themselves today, just as they did 5,000 years ago, in fundamentally similar images, plots, problems, and themes in the lives of individuals and cultures. A small-town insurance agent's dreams at 3:30 in the morning as he sleeps in his middle-class home in the suburbs of Denver may very well be paralleling the plots and characters in an ancient Sumerian myth. Clearly, concluded Jung, there was "a very deep psychosocial well from which individuals of all sorts, and cultures and religions of all times and all places, drew in order to produce the images, themes, and stories that expressed their ways of seeing and being in the world" (1953, 66). Jung called this "well" the *collective unconscious.*[6] Jung pictured this "very deep psychosocial well" metaphorically as different ripples, swirls, and patterns of energy that he called *archetypes*.

Approaching the Archetypes

The archetype is the most intriguing and powerful of all Jung's contributions to psychology—and it is also the most difficult to define. Indeed, most Jungians agree that—as with theoretical constructs in quantum physics—the idea of the archetype cannot really be *defined*. It can only be *approached* from a variety of angles, using various verbal formulations and even poetic images, in order to get an intuitive *sense* of what an archetype is.

A common way of picturing the archetypes is as inherent structures and predispositions at the deepest level of our psyches that cause us—despite personal and historical variations in language and imagery—to interpret and engage the world in much the same way from epoch to epoch and from culture to culture. As the bedrock of psychic functioning, they lie well beyond the limited reach of merely conscious awareness and even beyond the limited scope of the personal subconscious.

In functional terms, we might say that archetypes are the most powerful source of human creativity—at least, for those individuals who have the inclination and commitment to do the challenging inner work necessary in order to access them. They are "the inherited possibility of human imagination" (1953, 65), "typical modes of apprehension" (1960, 137). As inborn determinants of our higher psychological operations, they are the "spiritual" correlates of those physical instincts that determine our biological functions (1960, 138) and thus could be poetically pictured as the "image of instinct in man" (1968b, 179). Archetypes constitute "the *functional disposition* [of people throughout different times, places, and cultures] to produce the same, or very similar, ideas" (1956, 102. Emphasis added). Archetypes could also be characterized as "the stock of inherited *possibilities of representation* that are born anew in every individual" (1968a, 156).

Frey-Rohn's (1974, 92) excellent definition of archetypes has it that they are "preconscious categories which [channel] thought and action into definite shapes." Other Jungians have pictured archetypes as "a kind of mold for the accumulation and discharge of psychic energy" (Odajnyk 1976, 25) and speculated that they might actually *be* patterns of energy at the deepest and most formative levels of the psyche (143). As such, they are "irreducible and primary," "the structural nature of the psyche itself" (Palmer 1995, 8, 114). Jung and von Franz used a metaphor to characterize archetypes, comparing them to:

> the invisible potential existence of the crystalline structure in a saturated solution. [Archetypes] first take on a specific form when they emerge into consciousness in the shape of images; it is therefore necessary to differentiate between the unapprehendable archetype—the unconscious, preexistent disposition—and the archetypal images. [Archetypal images] are human nature in the universal sense. Myths and fairy tales are also characterized by this universal validity which differentiates them from ordinary dreams. (1986, 36–37)

Jung once discussed archetypes in theistic terms as the impulses, intuitions, longings, and fears that lie at the deepest level of psyche and soul. God has implanted them there, Jung averred, so that individuals and societies will strive to discover Him in their own personally and culturally unique ways (1977, 667).

It is highly important to note in any discussion of archetypes that they have both a light and a dark side, a conventionally "good" and conventionally "evil" side—although, as shown in the Jungian idea of the *shadow*, what seems to be "good" is not always (or not only) good, and what seems "bad" is not always or only bad. The light side of the Savior archetype, for instance, manifests itself in Jesus as the Redeemer from sin and error. Its dark side is Hitler, who, claiming to be the savior of a nation and a race, stimulated and constellated the shadow side of this archetype in an entire people, leading them into sin and error, not saving them from it.

I would offer the following as a "definition" of the collective unconscious and its archetypes. The collective unconscious is the dynamic psychic matrix from which all our other psychic functioning—conscious and subconscious, light and dark—emerges. The collective unconscious is composed of the archetypes, which can be pictured metaphorically as constantly interacting, occasionally overlapping, and subtly morphing "patterns of energy." Through the archetypes, we interpret and shape our subjective and objective worlds in a distinctly human manner that has, in the most essential ways, remained fairly constant throughout history and across cultures. How an individual experiences and uses archetypal energy is variable, depending largely upon her native health, character, and personal experiences as well as upon the many cultural factors, past and present, that have shaped her—cultural factors that are themselves, in large measure, the products of collective archetypal processes. The collective unconscious is the place where human consciousness and transcendent consciousness intersect. As such, the collective unconscious exists not only "inside the head" of a person, but is woven into the fabric of the universe itself.

COMMON ARCHETYPES

Some of the most common archetypes are: the Trickster, Lover, Divine Child, Magical Animal, Nurturing Mother, Witch, the Law-giving Father, Senex (i.e., stern old man), the Prince of Darkness, the Savior, Ritual Sacrifice, initiation, matrimony, trinities and quaternities, judgment, heaven, hell, and atonement. There are a great many others. These archetypes are activated (or, to use the Jungian term, "constellated") by typical life-situations that occur in all cultures: birth, the child's relationship to its parents and siblings, puberty, courtship, marriage, vocation, aging and death, and so on.

A crucial point, however, often missed in discussions of Jungian psychology is that *even though archetypes are universal, archetypal images are not.* This is the case because archetypal images are the specific stories, personages, and images that a particular individual in a particular society in a particular time and place will produce to express the universal, transcendent energy of the archetype. Archetypal images are, as it were, the "incarnations" in personally, historically, and culturally specific "clothing" of naked, universal, archetypal energies. Take, for example, the archetype of "The Trickster," which is found in all cultures. In Native American culture, The Trickster incarnates in the image of the wily prankster Coyote. In ancient Irish culture, The Trickster manifests itself as mischievous fairies. An actual person can also embody Trickster energy for a culture—as, for instance, President Bill Clinton did for many people in his ability to get into and out of any jam with his "tricky" use of words. "It all depends," he once said, "on what your definition of 'is' is."

Anima AND *Animus*

Two of the most important of all the archetypes are the *anima* and the *animus*. Anima is the feminine form of the Latin word for "soul" and animus is the masculine form. Jung introduced into modern psychology the idea that every man has an inner feminine component, and that every woman has an inner masculine component. He believed that as an individual begins to move past mere ego consciousness into the realm of spirit, his or her dreams will be increasingly populated by especially compelling figures of the opposite sex—figures that symbolize the "soul-level" of psyche. This is the case, Jung felt, because woman is typically the primary, mysterious "other" for man, just as man generally plays the same role for most women.

It should not be surprising, therefore, that the individual psyche approaching the mysterious threshold of the transpersonal realm should be greeted in dreams and fantasies by a figure of the opposite sex, promising adventure and symbolizing the soul. For a man, those dream and fantasy images are embodiments of the archetype of the anima (the male's inner feminine) and the animus (the female's inner male). Jung also felt that when a man is romantically attracted to a person of the opposite sex (whether in a dream or waking life), what largely accounts for that attraction (whatever else may be happening at the simply sexual level, of course) is that the attractive person is an embodiment of contrasexual archetypal energy for the admirer—of the anima for a man and of the animus for a woman.

Learning how to integrate one's anima or animus is a major task of Jungian therapy. It is an absolute requirement of *individuation*—or psychospiritual maturation, balance, and completeness. This is true for two reasons. First, if we do not acknowledge the contrasexual elements in our individual psyches, we will tend to project them onto someone else. Jung felt that many marital problems, for instance, are caused by the husband inappropriately projecting his mythical anima figure, the internal goddess of his soul who symbolizes passion and intuition, onto his all-too-mortal wife. A woman does the same thing with her very fallible husband when she expects him to be the knight in shining armor—an archetypal image of a transpersonal reality which, in fact, truly exists at the center of her own soul as the potential source of power and clarity.

Second, said Jung, if we do not consciously face and incorporate our contrasexual energies into our complete psychic functioning, then those energies will, like any repressed energies, "rebel" and assert themselves in overbearing and unhealthy ways. Men who will not examine and embrace their inner feminine, can not creatively possess their animas but will instead become *anima possessed*. When this happens, a man begins to look like a caricature of the archetypally feminine principle—snappy, sloppily sentimental, given to erratic moods, bitchy. Conversely, *animus possessed* women start looking like caricatures of the archetypally masculine principle—opinionated, stubborn, and caught in twisted webs of ambition and pseudologic.

The Shadow, Persona, and Projection

For all of his focus on the transpersonal dimension of psychic functioning, Jung never lost sight of the psyche's *personal* nature—its strictly biographical dimension. For instance, Jung coined the psychological term *persona* to refer to the ego-protecting façade that we don for others to see. Having *personas* is not in itself a bad thing. It is, in fact, a very necessary thing, for the persona "mediates between the ego and the outer world" (Samuels 1997, 215). Problems regarding the persona arise when it no longer functions as the ego's servant but becomes its master, resulting in a false personality (Jung 1921, 425). When a person begins to define herself by the social masks she wears, she is no longer in control of them. They are in control of her. She becomes inauthentic to herself and others, which leads to neurosis.

Another Jungian contribution to ego-psychology is the idea of the *shadow*. "By *shadow* I mean the negative side of the personality—the sum of all those unpleasant qualities we like to hide, together with the insufficiently developed functions, and the contents of the personal unconscious" (Jung 1953, 66, n. 5). Many people incorrectly take Jung's idea of the shadow to mean that it is simply the awful repository of all that is evil in us. To be sure, the Jungian shadow does contain much that is evil, for we do not like to see evil in ourselves. But evil is not banished to the shadow so much because it is evil as because it is something *we prefer not to acknowledge as belonging to us*. Hence, repressed memories are also in the shadow. So are "qualities we like to hide." These qualities may actually be quite positive—talents, virtues, or potentials that we have hidden not only from others, but from ourselves, because openly acknowledging them could place us in emotional or social peril. Also residing in the shadow are certain "insufficiently developed functions."

It is important to confront the shadow because many things that one has repressed can, if consciously acknowledged and carefully nurtured, emerge from the shadow and help a person become more complete, powerful, and whole—in a word, more individuated. There is yet another reason that we must confront our own shadows, and it has to do with another concept from Jungian psychology that has become widely known: *Projection*. If we refuse to consciously and constructively face our own shadows, we will unconsciously and destructively project them onto others. This is simply another way of stating the old adage that "we hate most in others what we refuse to look at in ourselves."

In dreams, the shadow is usually the same gender as the dreamer and often has something dark associated with it. The dream character might have a dark complexion and/or dark hair (a fact which not infrequently seems to be as true for people of color as for Caucasians); the figure may be wearing dark clothes; sometimes he or she is literally standing in or peeking out of a shadow. The fact that the shadow has been "despised" by consciousness can also be symbolized in either dream- or waking-consciousness in the form of aliens, citizens of an opposing country, members of a minority group, criminals, or beggars; or by characters who seem unethical, sick, or menacing. Some racism results from shadow projection (Adams 1996).

PERSONALITY TYPES[7]

In his study of ancient literature, science, and medicine, Jung had often noted the importance of four-pointed symmetrical forms—quaternities—to many great thinkers, who saw in it the structural core of everything from the human body to the cosmos. Jung thus concluded that the quaternity was an archetypal form. Jung pointed out that quaternities often were comprised of two paired opposites within a whole—a cross within a circle, a "unification of a double dyad" (1968c).

Jung's interest in the phenomenon was primarily clinical, for many of his patients reported dreams that had quaternities—both imagistically, in the form of four-chambered mandalas, and thematically, in the form of characters who "squared off" as paired opposites. Observing that his patients seemed to divide into four basic personality types, which he called the thinking, feeling, sensate, and intuitive types, Jung further categorized these types into two sets of paired opposites: thinking/feeling and sensate/intuitive. Wishing to avoid simplistic interpretations of his theory, Jung was quick to add that everyone had elements of all four of these ways of interacting with the world within himself. Furthermore, he insisted that no personality type was intrinsically better than the other three. Each was simply a different way of engaging with the world, and each had its own peculiar strengths and weaknesses. Although no one should be schematically reduced to just *one* psychological function, most people tend to use one particular function more than the others, which, Jung said, can be identified as that person's *superior function*—the opposite of his *inferior function*, which is typically banished to the shadow. Knowing what a person's superior function is can be therapeutically useful. It can also be educationally useful.

To complete his typological system, Jung added a final dimension—that of the *attitudes*. There are two fundamental attitudes: *introversion* and *extroversion*, popular terms which originated with Jung. The four functions times the two attitudes yields eight basic personality types.

Introversion is:

> an inward turning of *libido*, in the sense of a negative relation to the object. Interest does not move toward the object, but withdraws from it into the subject. Everyone whose attitude is introverted thinks, feels, and acts in a way that clearly demonstrates that the subject is the prime motivating factor and that the object is of secondary importance. (1921, 452–453)

Conversely, *extroversion* is:

> an outward turning of *libido*, I use this concept to denote a manifest relation of subject to object, a positive movement

> of subjective interest toward the object [an "object"in this case being not only a thing, but also a situation, event, or person]. Everyone in the extraverted state thinks, feels, and acts in relation to the object, and moreover in a direct and clearly observable fashion, so that no doubt can remain about his positive dependence on the object. In a sense, therefore, extroversion is a transfer of interest from subject to object. (1921, 481-482)

Just as each of the four major types must be thought of only as a tendency, introversion and extroversion must be seen as ways of relating to the external world that are "habitual," but by no means exclusive.

The popular Myers-Briggs Type Indicator was devised on Jungian principles. Gardner's (1983) theory of multiple intelligences also contains elements of Jungian typology. Indeed, many currently popular devices for categorizing personality can be traced back to Jung's seminal work in typology. Jungian typology has been quite influential in educational research and practice, especially in identifying and improving teachers' and students' styles of relating to each other and the curriculum.

Cultural Aspects of Jungian Psychology

Jungian psychology has been accused of being apolitical, lost in some mystical inner realm where there is no awareness of or concern for society. However, a good deal of recent research extends and applies Jungian ideas to political and cultural issues, showing how these were always present in, and indeed an important part of, Jung's vision of the psyche (Adams 1996; Gray 1996).

Jung's sociocultural message was always that members of a society should be aware of and honor the sacred narratives and normative values that underlie their culture. "Anything new should always be questioned and tested with caution, for it may very easily turn out to be only a new disease" (1954, 145). He detested "the present tendency," which he saw in the excessive materialism of both socialism and capitalism, "to destroy all tradition or render it unconscious," for such demythologizing of life strips human life of its dignity and sacredness (1968b, 181). Furthermore, we can comprehend ourselves deeply and resist attempts at political domination—from either the Right or the Left—only by a solid appreciation of our past. This is why "loss of roots and lack of tradition neuroticize the masses and prepare them for collective hysteria" (1968b, 181).

Unlike many people who argue culturally conservative points, however, Jung did not do so out of a sense of cultural superiority. A great student of culture, from the nearest to the most distant in space and time, Jung traveled from the jungles of Africa to the deserts of New Mexico to gain first-hand experience of First Nation peoples, about whom he wrote with genuine admiration that sometimes bordered on envy. Hence, there is a lifetime of personal and intellectual experience in Jung's pithy observation—which ran quite counter to the political views that were quite fashionable in Europe and the United States during Jung's time—that "the white race is not a species of *homo sapiens* specially favored by God" (1954, 82).

Another political implication of Jungian psychology is Jung's belief that the idea of the shadow and projection could help members of a culture examine their culture's darker side. For just as individuals have shadows which they tend to project onto others, so do societies (Odajnyk 1976). Jung also exerted a palpable influence on twentieth century gender politics in his insistence that the feminine principle must be honored equally with the male principle, and that, indeed, the two must be brought into balance, within both the individual and society—an idea that figures prominently in the chapters that follow.

In the final analysis, personal and sociocultural issues are inseparably blended in Jungian psychology. Jung constantly asserted that our personal identities are so bound up with our collective histories that we cannot know ourselves as individuals if we do not also understand ourselves as members of a culture that rests on foundational mythic narratives. This is how June Singer (1988, xi) has explained the fact that the texts and subtexts of the narratives that a person constructs regarding his or her life and work often have such clear archetypal images and motifs. These "personal mythologies," as she calls them, "are not false beliefs. They are not the stories you tell yourself to explain your circumstances and behavior. Your personal mythology is, rather, the vibrant infrastructure that informs your life, whether or not you are aware of it. Consciously and unconsciously, you live by your mythology"—a mythology whose images and patterns, problems and potentials, rest upon cultural narratives that have themselves emerged from the universal collective unconscious.

For many people, then, profound reflectivity about their life, love, and work is immeasurably enriched by moving into the archetypal dimension. Indeed, as we are about to see, The Hero's myth, one of the most universal and potent of the products of the collective unconscious, will transport us swiftly into the archetypal dimension, serving us well in our attempt to reflect on some of the deeper psycho-spiritual mysteries of teaching and learning.

Notes

1. The examination of depth and transpersonal psychology in this chapter is largely drawn from my article, "The psychoanalytic view of education: 1922–2002" *Journal of Curriculum Studies,* 49(1), 539-567, and from my book *Inside Education: Depth Psychology in Teaching and Learning* (2007), Atwood Publishing. I am grateful to Atwood and *The Journal of Curriculum Studies* for their permission to use that material in this chapter.

2. As with so much else in Freudian psychology, however, it is well to remember that Freud's ideas stem from historical roots and did not simply appear out of nowhere. The early Mesmerists, Magnetists, and other proto-psychiatrists, for instance, had noted the potentially dangerous phenomenon of the patient's growing attraction (often of a sexual nature) to the clinician, as well as the patient's identification of the clinician with someone from the past (Ellenberger 1970).

3. Not many Freudians shared then, however, and not all share even now, this positive view of the possibilities of the counter-transference. For example, Winnicott, an important psychoanalytic theorist and therapist, has tersely restated the classical Freudian position that "the meaning of the word *counter-transference* can only be the [analyst's] neurotic features *that spoil the professional attitude* and disturb the course of the analytic process as determined by the patient" (1988, 266). This, however, is rapidly becoming the minority view in the neo-Freudian literature on the counter-transference. Winnicott's disinclination to consider counter-transference a valid part of the therapeutic process may have been due to the fact that his work was primarily with children, who, because they are particularly vulnerable, certainly have a special need to be protected against harmful counter-transferences from the analyst.

4. The reader who is interested in getting a solid overview of modern developments in psychoanalytic theory might want to begin with Eagle's excellent (1993) study, *Recent Developments in Psychoanalysis: A Critical Evaluation*.

5. This idea has come under fire recently from some theorists who believe that the child has a sense of its mother as a distinct person, and not just an extension of himself, virtually from the first moments of conscious awareness (Wade 1996).

6. It should be borne in mind that the collective unconscious is a theoretical construct and not some definite place inside the brain or floating around in the cosmos, although it undoubtedly does have physiological components and astral dimensions.

7. Although I am subsuming Jungian typology under Jung's ego psychology, it must be kept in mind that there are certainly archetypal aspects of the issue of one's personality type. However, since the superior function is one's primary way of dealing with the world and, furthermore, since one's inferior function usually is primarily a shadow issue, it seems sensible to discuss personality as primarily an ego function.

CHAPTER 2

Issuing the Call

The problem and promise of change

A culture's ethical and legal systems grow out of the fertile matrix of the culture's sacred stories. Sacred stories make up the foundation of a society (Bruner 1996). And at the very center of many culturally foundational stories is the mythical hero who, passing through trials and temptations, embodies a culture's idea of the good. Examples of such heroes in the major religious stories come easily to mind—Jesus, the Buddha, Moses, and Mohammed. Familiar heroes in national myths include Abraham Lincoln, Rosa Parks, Martin Luther King, and Mahatma Gandhi. Other culture heroes range from figures as diverse as Mother Teresa and Luke Skywalker. In each case, the hero has power and charisma—what the Oceanic cultures call *mana*—because his story illustrates what a culture believes to be sacred, reminds the reader or listener of what has degenerated in her own personal and cultural life, and introduces new and revitalizing ideas. And since appropriating and acting on eternal truths is (or arguably should be) *everyone's* goals in life, the hero and his journey are ultimately symbols of everyone's unique trek through mortality in search of truth. Embodying what we wish to become, the hero universally embodies each person's unique quest for the Light.

Thus, according to Jung, the Hero's Journey symbolizes the psychospiritual process of each person's individuation. Individuation means "[to become] an individual being, in so far as we understand by individuality our innermost, ultimate, and incomparable uniqueness" (see Goldbrunner 1964, 94). A human being is not just a very intelligent animal driven by primal instincts. She is more than merely a biological machine whose behavior is totally determined by positive and negative reinforcements. Rather, her psyche is "essentially a self-organizing entity stirring to continually unfold some innate destiny factor"—which is an apt characterization of both the process of individuation and the course of the Hero's Journey (Conforti 1999, 112).

Individuation is the individual finding and internalizing eternal realities in her own way, and, in so doing, perhaps becoming eternal herself.

Superficial readers of Jung sometimes confuse individuation with mere "individualism." In fact, these two things are quite opposite. Individualism cares little for others and is rarely motivated by any goals higher than the crass ones of flaunting superficial personal differences or brashly defending personal turf. Individuation, on the other hand, is the very antithesis of the narcissistic messages that scream out at us from every direction in contemporary culture. Individuation is the sacred life-task that the Eternal lays upon us all as human beings: to appropriate universal truths in a personal way within the context of a particular culture.

The heroic journey of individuation represents nothing less than the quest for "self realization and wholeness"—one's ongoing ethical evolution into the best that one can be in order to be of the greatest emotional, intellectual, social, and spiritual benefit to one's fellow beings. Naturally, individuation does not happen at some definite point in one's life—just as the initiate does not become a hero in a single moment. Individuation is life itself—the continuous process of growing existentially. It goes on until the very moment of death, and, in my faith-tradition, continues even beyond death—in an eternal dynamic of personal progression. As such it is a never-ending shaping of oneself as an artistic work-in-progress, "an ongoing creation" (Pauson 1988, 61).

I believe that this is what the British philosopher Alfred North Lord Whitehead meant when he proclaimed that "all true education is religious" (Whitehead 1967, 69). He did not mean that education should attempt to convert a student to a particular religious system—or even to religion, as such, at all. What Whitehead meant is that all true education should have as its central purpose the nurturance of the student in her heroic journey to individuation—to meaning, purpose, and hope—whether she is studying physics or physical education, computer science or comparative literature, botany or band. When education operates in the service of individuation, it is what I call "*transformative education*." The Hero's Journey is thus a fitting symbol for what teaching and learning as existential transformation should basically be about. Just as the Hero's Journey is essentially an educative one, so the educational process should essentially be a heroic one—a striving for individuation through the medium of the curriculum and in the context of the classroom.

"The Call to Adventure": Refusal and Acceptance

The Hero's Journey begins with a call to adventure, which a person may either heed or not heed. If a person does not heed the call to adventure, the consequences—both in life and in myth—are dire.

> Often in actual life, and not infrequently in myths and popular tales, we encounter the dull case of the call unanswered; it is always possible to turn the ear to other interests. Refusal of the summons converts the adventure into its negative. Walled in by boredom, hard work, or "culture," the subject loses the power of significant affirmative action and becomes a victim to be saved. His flowering world becomes a wasteland of dry stones and his life feels meaningless—even though, like King Minos, he may through titanic effort succeed in building an empire of renown. Whatever house he builds, it will be a house of death. . . . All he can do is create new problems for himself and await the gradual approach of his disintegration. (Campbell 1949, 59)

In this section I examine two of the basic reasons why a student may not respond to the call to educational adventure. The first is that the student is compelled to respond to a false call that is imposed on her from without. The second reason originates more from within the student, having to do with psychodynamic issues that cause her to resist a true call to deep existential transformation.

The False Call: Schooling as Corporate Anti-Adventure

To define the ultimate goals of education in lesser terms than those offered by Whitehead is a mistake. When education is primarily oriented around functionality and not transformation, then (to repeat Campbell's warning) "the adventure [turns] into its negative." As the noted curriculum theorist Duane Huebner asserted: "The journey of the self is short circuited or derailed by those who define the ends of life and education in less than ultimate terms" (1999, 404). "It cannot be the aim of education," Jung warned, "to turn out rationalists, materialists, specialists, technicians, and others of the kind who, unconscious of their origins, are precipitated abruptly into the present and contribute to the disorientation and fragmentation of society" (cited in Frey-Rohn 1974, 182). Such pseudo-education exists simply to service the needs of a consumer society and to support the growth of its military-fiscal machinery. It is not really education at all in the sense that I wish to use that term. It is "training." In education for ultimacy, on the other hand, almost any subject matter may become an occasion for the revelation of Self in tolerant and mutually edifying relationship with others.

Of course, it would be snobbish and unrealistic to argue that there is no place in our schools and universities for technical training to address the practical issues of everyday life, for this is one of the important secondary purposes of education. However, it should never be a primary purpose in a society's definition of its educational goals. When technical education *does* usurp the role of a culture's primary educational purposes—as, for example, has been the case historically in corporate educational agendas like *A Nation at Risk* (National Commission on Excellence in Education 1983) and *No Child Left Behind* (The No Child Left Behind Act of 2002), which value education only insofar as it promotes a nation's military and industrial might—then education degenerates into training.

The false call to pseudo-education issued by the proponents of the corporate state is not only anti-heroic, but also anti-democratic. It does not aim at helping young people think deeply about the fundamental questions with which the citizens of a viable democracy must constantly be grappling—questions such as the following:

> What are the best ways to promote social and economic justice in our society? How can we attain a balance in spending between the legitimate needs for self-defense and the pressing needs of those who live on the margins and require social programs to help them better their conditions? How can we make our cities into aesthetically attractive zones of ethical commerce? How can we as a people learn to create and enjoy art that expresses our most authentic experiences and our highest ideals as a diverse people? And, in general, what values should we embrace in order to make our individual and communal lives as beautiful, humane, and creative as possible?

Corporate education tends to look with a suspicious eye at education that delves too deeply into such political and ethical topics. These questions, and the answers they yield, often involve critique of and resistance to existing power structures. This is precisely what corporate education wishes to avoid, for it requires obedience to "the organization" in the service of military and fiscal growth at virtually any human cost. Corporate education does not educate people to critique the dominant system; it trains them to unreflectively take their place within the system. When this occurs, schooling degenerates into a means—in many ways, the primary means—of spawning a docile and dull citizenry, ready to be controlled by any party of powermongers who wave a flag, mouth empty patriotic platitudes, and are able (largely through schools and the media) to instill every possible variety of false consciousness into the heads of the people.

I wish to stress again, however, that technical training—whether that training has to do with fixing a car or fixing a failing business—has its legitimate and important place in a culture's educational systems. Every student benefits from such training and, as Dewey (1916) insisted, all students should get it. In fact, vocational education in the United States began, in the opening years of the twentieth century, as a way of teaching all students a wide variety of technical skills, and also of instilling respect for such work in the minds and hearts of all students, whether or not they ultimately wound up doing such work for a living (Cremin 1964). It was thus seen as important that *every* student experience technical training of some sort, so that vocational education would not become an academic ghetto.

Nevertheless, this ghettoizing effect is exactly what has occurred in the United States. "Voc Ed" has functioned largely as an academic dumping ground where we tend to send young people from lower socioeconomic groups (Apple 1990; Bowles and Gintis 1976; Kantor 1988; Oakes 2000). In this and other ways, American schooling too often perpetuates socioeconomic injustices that are anathema to a democracy, instead of working to eradicate them. Technical training has its place—one in which a student after a certain age might, if she chooses, remain for as long as she genuinely believes that it best suits her talents and purposes to do so. But it must be approached cautiously, implemented fairly and universally, and never become the central feature of a nation's educational system.

It should come as no surprise that the proponents of the uncritical, technical approach to education should advocate for standardized instruction and assessment, for it is only the results of technical training that *can* be measured on a standardized test. By definition, there will never be a standardized test capable of doing even the slightest justice to the intangible, unquantifiable, and delicate transformations of consciousness and emotion that *transformative education* promotes. Thus, when standardized instruction and assessment become of primary importance in an educational system, we may be certain that

that system has lost the heroic vision of schooling, in which the primary emphasis is always on the student as a hero in her journey towards personal meaning, cultural relevance and social critique, and ethical renewal. Where training takes precedence over education in defining a culture's essential educational aims, schooling begins to serve anti-heroic and anti-educational purposes. It stops the student dead in her existential tracks—to ultimately sacrifice her on a high-tech altar of various corporate agendas. It entices her into a counterfeit quest in search of the mock Grails of money, status, and power.

Whether those seductive corporate agendas are of the "neo-conservative" or "neo-liberal" variety makes little difference. The message in both cases echoes the same old song sung by the authors of that dismal twentieth century manifesto of corporate education, *A Nation at Risk,* whose authors declared that "the basic purposes of schooling" is to reassert America's "once unchallenged preeminence in commerce, industry, science, and technological innovation." Only these economically and politically hegemonic goals counted. All others were seen, at best, as merely "frills." This is the "vision" of education that is increasingly shaping not only our public schools, but our universities as well (Giroux and Myrcieades 2001).

In sum, instead of being nurtured and enlarged by the journey of schooling, the student's talents and potentials that do not fall within the rigid guidelines of the corporate blueprint are suppressed, even erased, by the mechanisms of standardized instruction and assessment. Gaining insight and cultivating creativity are sacrificed to memorizing disconnected facts in areas of study that are themselves disconnected from each other. The student, to be "successful," registers one lesson above all others: "Abandon your better self—and conform!" And hanging always over her head to reinforce this message is the big stick of the high-stakes test.

MARX'S THREE TYPES OF ALIENATION AND GIDDENS'S THREE SITES OF CORPORATE POWER

Marx (1978) believed that in societies such as ours that are obsessed by the accumulation of objects, the individual is ultimately turned into just another object herself. She becomes a cog in the corporate machine. Because of this objectification of the individual, Marx observed, she suffers three existential wounds of alienation. These wounds are increasingly visible in teachers and students.

The first is *alienation from one's work*. In educational terms, this means that one's work does not grow out of one's deepest values and needs, but is imposed upon both teacher and student to service someone else's agenda of control. In all my years of being a teacher and studying teachers, I have never yet met one who said that she became a teacher because, "I am passionate about helping students get higher scores on standardized tests!" Teachers typically take on their difficult job because they love students, because they want to instill ethical and civic virtues in students, and also because they wish to communicate the excitement that they feel about their subject-matter (Lortie 1975).

The second type of alienation in corporate society is *alienation from others*. Having become an object of a dehumanizing system, the individual begins to view and treat others as objects, too—objects with whom one is in constant competition. This runs quite counter to the need that most teachers feel to nurture students as unique *subjects,* not regimented objects, and to promote their holistic growth. The depersonalizing of the teacher-student relationship in corporate education deprives teachers of their greatest source of satisfaction: the joy of a deepening relationship with students—the teacher's all-important "psychic reward" for her demanding and often financially and socially undervalued work (Lortie 1975).

Objectification and excessive competition also destroy the heroic educational ideal of a vibrant community of mutually respectful dialogue in the classroom. Dewey (1916) saw this as crucial to the maintenance of democracy, for in learning how to be a member of a democratic classroom, a student would learn the larger lesson of what it means to be a responsible member of a democracy. The classroom should be a *laboratory of democracy*, as Dewey was fond of putting it. It should be where students learn to formulate interesting questions together, cooperate in creating the ideas and tools to address those questions, and then build upon their shared achievements as a community of discourse to generate a new set of questions, tasks, and tools. This is education for both independence and interdependence. Corporate education, on the other hand, trains the student out of her individuality, away from curiosity, and away from rich relationships with her teacher and fellow students. These are precluded by the constant pressure to prepare for the big test and its ethos of zero-sum competition on those tests, where my high ranking on the bell-curve of the distribution of scores implies your low ranking, and vice versa.

Marx's third form of alienation is *the individual's ultimate alienation from herself as a subject, a truly* human *being*. Alienated from her work and from vibrant relationship with her fellows, she is no longer a subject-for-herself or a subject-with-others, but an object-among-objects. In the corporate classroom, the student is essentially seen as "human capital"—a political and pedagogical "unit" to be micromanaged, measured, and cultivated for maximum financial gain. As the great Marxist pedagogue Paolo Freire (1970) insisted, the student in a materialist, corporate society becomes just another investment by the corporate elite in its hegemonic future. This is what he called the "banking model" of education.

According to the British sociologist Anthony Giddens, the power of the new corporate elite (and the source of the false call to the pseudo-education of the "banking model") exists in three distinct yet interdependent sites of power: (1) the new corporate state and its rapidly growing, increasingly subtle use of electronic means of surveillance, (2) the growth of transnational corporate capitalism, enabled by the advent and proliferation of new communication technologies, and (3) the new world-military order (Giddens 2002). It is, I believe, this postmodern military–fiscal complex (or one like it) that is increasingly commandeering our educational systems.

Cremin's (1988) military–industrial–educational complex is just on the horizon. The battle between the opposing visions of education-as-heroic versus education-as-corporatist reflects a larger social crisis as corporatism and conformity increasingly consume democracy and critique. Indeed, it is no exaggeration to say that this educational battle not only reflects this crisis, but that its outcome may well play a role in how the larger battle turns out. As educators, we therefore have not only the pedagogical responsibility to teach heroically and transformatively. We have the political and ethical responsibility to do so.

PSYCHO-CULTURAL FACTORS IN ACCEPTING OR REFUSING THE CALL

So far in this chapter, I have focused on the corporate threat to the heroic vision of education. But there are also psychodynamic issues, often deeply intertwined with a student's cultural commitments, which act against her responding positively to an authentic call to educational adventure.

A student's resistance to schooling is sometimes not only understandable, but quite healthy if the curriculum and instruction are oppressive. Indeed, it is precisely this kind of resistance—and not only by students, but also by teachers—that I am trying to provoke in the above section, and indeed throughout the book, for, along with Postman and Weingartner (1969), I see teaching as a "subversive activity." But resistance is not healthy when what a student is resisting are new avenues of inquiry and experimentation that could help to open up her world. This amounts to a refusal of the call to educational adventure, and, as noted at the beginning of this chapter, such a refusal, in both the classroom and life in general, can have seriously negative consequences for the person. "His flowering world becomes a wasteland of dry stones and his life feels meaningless" (Campbell 1949, 59). Let us examine some of the major psychodynamic issues involved in why a student might refuse a call to authentic educational adventure.

By definition, education as a heroic journey changes a student. But change is precisely what the ego—lodged in its defenses, relying upon the tranquilizing predictability of its surroundings, and resting upon unquestioned cultural norms—typically wants to resist. Transformative education invites the student to reexamine, and sometimes reject, habitual ego-defenses and conceptual-structures, as well as internalized cultural norms. Understandably, this may be threatening to the student, for it requires critical encounter with one's belief-system(s)—from casual assumptions (usually not too difficult to relinquish) to convictions that go to the student's very core (which are very hard to relinquish, modify, or even simply question). It should not be too surprising to teachers, therefore, that pushing the envelope beyond the student's present worldview may inspire in the student existential dread, a fear of psycho-cultural death.

After all, our worldviews are our source of comfort, orientation, and identity. Our beliefs tell us who we are, what the world is, how it works, and what our place in it should be. Our beliefs are the living bricks out of which our ego-structures are largely constructed. For this reason, the student may easily construe the invitation to modify her worldview not as an invitation, but a deathly threat—at least to that part of the ego that was so heavily invested in its newly challenged commitments. Wherever there is the threat of death, the individual instinctively deploys her best defenses to meet it. "If I allow some (and perhaps many) of my basic commitments to change, even be rejected for new ones, then what will happen to my world and my idea of its basic operating rules, my relationship with people whom I love, the ways in which I have defined and deal with 'others' who are strange to me, the manner in which I interpret my past and anticipate my future, and, in general, my idea of self, society, nature, and God?" Learning is a high-stakes existential gamble.

Every teacher has experienced resistance from students and knows how exasperating it can be. Yet, the exasperated teacher would do well to remember that not only her students, but everyone, including herself, tends to resist new paradigms—and they tend to do so with a degree of stubbornness that is directly proportional to the seriousness of the threat that the new paradigm poses. This is why conceptual-change theorists (who study why a student's ideas about something either do or do not change after instruction) have correctly insisted over the last 15 or so years that cognition is "hot" (Pintrich, Marx, and Boyle 1993).

The fact that cognition is hot means that the sets of ideas that a student brings to class about a topic or even an entire field of study are not just an assemblage of logical conclusions that she has made throughout her life and duly recorded. They are, rather, the complex and passionate fruit of her personal, familial, and cultural engagements with life. In other words, a student's beliefs are rarely ever "cold"—so detached from her total being that they can be managed at will by a teacher through the simple presentation of some interesting new evidence, citation of an impressive source, or even the teacher's eloquent rhetoric.

Nevertheless, the idea that cognition is "cold" informed much early research in conceptual change theory. Some of the earliest researchers in this field, such as Posner and his associates (1982), assumed that students change concepts and constructs in much the same way that scientists are believed to do. Posner laid out four stages that (so he and his colleagues assumed) accurately described how conceptual change occurs in scientists, and therefore should occur in students: (1) dissatisfaction with existing conceptions, usually because of the appearance of new data that do not fit into the old conceptions, (2) intelligibility of a new conception, (3) plausibility of the new conception, and (4) fruitfulness of the new conception in experimental trials.

There were four pedagogical imperatives that seemed to Posner and his associates to follow from all this. The teacher should: (1) create cognitive conflicts in the students by the Socratic method, (2) diagnose students' errors and defenses, (3) increase her repertoire of strategies to deal with her students' errors and defenses, and (4) learn how to be a model of scientific thinking for her students. By this view, effective pedagogy was essentially the "scientific method" tailored to the exigencies of the classroom. Despite their strengths, such methods of instruction are not without their problems. For, not only do *students* not change their concepts like scientists do—even *scientists* do not change their concepts like scientists do—if by a "scientist" we mean a completely dispassionate person, one who has no emotional, cultural, institutional, religious, or anti-religious investment in a certain theory being "true" and another one being "false." Such a grotesque caricature of a human being has probably never existed—at least, one hopes not!

In a work that revolutionized how we think about how scientists think, *The Structure of Scientific Revolutions*, Thomas Kuhn (1970) studied how fundamental shifts in scientific paradigms in the history of Western science have typically occurred not because a scientist, confronted with strange data, dutifully used "the scientific method" to form a new hypothesis, which he then tested out to see if it would account for the new data. Rather, radical changes in scientific assumptions—regarding everything from the structure of the atom to the existence of other time-space continua—have occurred because a certain scientist or group of scientists have chosen *to ask fundamentally different questions* about the world. These new questions will (like the old questions) be rooted in personal, cultural, and historical factors. Kuhn called such changes "paradigm shifts"—a phrase that has found its way into popular speech.

Indeed, it is arguable that in many instances, scientific theories rest more upon poetic imagery than anything else. Einstein got his first inklings of the theory of relativity not as an adult physicist coldly considering the weakness of the "luminiferous aether" theory of the propagation of sound waves. Rather, as a little boy he simply used to wonder what it would be like to ride on a beam of light through space! In a sense, his entire scientific career was a complex conceptual articulation of a radically simple and breathtakingly beautiful poetic image—sporting on the head of a beam of light as it raced through space.

The history of science is filled with examples of poetic intuition and imagery providing the foundation upon which a system has then arisen according to its own internal, intuitive logic. For instance, there is von Stadonitz's dream of the ends of swirling molecules bending and touching to form a ring (similar to the image of intertwining snakes—an archetypal picture of psychospiritual energy that appears in sources as diverse as Kundalini Yoga, Gnostic Christianity, and the modern physician's caduceus). This poetic dream image set the stage for the empirical discovery of the double-helix in biology. And the great mathematician Poincaré claimed that all of his major theories began as poetic images stirring in his soul.

Emotions and emotionally charged imagery are always a part, and sometimes the most important part, of any "concept." Salzberger-Wittenberg (1989) has thus correctly insisted that a pedagogy which ignores "*the emotional experience* of teaching and learning" will probably not only be ineffective, but may finally prove to be quite damaging to the student. Cold, dry presentations of facts in an emotional vacuum leads, at best, to some very unpleasant classroom hours for students, and may even permanently douse whatever fire of interest in a subject may have existed for the student at the beginning of the term. Only the threat of "the test" and "the final grade" are barbed enough to whip the student into temporary submission—a strategic "surrender" on the student's part. As soon as the term has ended, the same student either forgets or actively repudiates the "knowledge" that was dictatorially beaten into her in the prison-camp of the classroom.

Where the threat of punitive testing exists in all its toxicity in the classroom, a student's psychological dynamics and cultural commitments may still be sufficiently strong to enable her to refuse to be bullied into abandoning her beliefs—even if her resistance results in a bad grade or a "ruined professional future." In the sociology of education, this phenomenon has been documented in a wide variety of learning environments—from kindergarten to grad school—by Henry Giroux in a model of academic failure known as "Resistance Theory" (1983).

Where the threat to the student's psychic and/or cultural identity is also felt by other students in the classroom who have the same sets of commitments, they will often band together in common cause, creating peer-groups of resistance both inside and outside the classroom (Deyhle 1986; MacLeod 1987). These groups also put pressure on other students to engage in (anti-)scholastic guerilla warfare in the classroom to undermine the teacher and institution. In these cases, failing grades are not seen by students as damning evidence of their "intellectual weakness," but are proudly displayed as "medals" commemorating their resistance to a psychologically insensitive teacher and a culturally oppressive curriculum (Wax, Wax, and Dumont 1964).

A teacher's authoritarian attempts to force impersonal "concepts and evidence" upon a student may also cause the student to twist and turn those concepts and pieces of evidence in such a way that they wind up supporting her preexisting beliefs. I teach multicultural theory. As anyone who has ever taught this subject knows, a student may so persistently misinterpret the readings and lectures during a term that at the end of the term she is more prejudiced than before (Devine 1995; Garner 1990). Sometimes a student's prejudices must be confronted harshly, head-on. It has been my experience, however, teaching multicultural theory to both undergraduates and graduates at a conservative religious university, that a student's misconceptions must often be approached with tact and even a certain degree of gentle humor in order to effect any deep and lasting change in them.

Chinn and Brewer (1993) have provided a useful taxonomy of how a student resists new ideas, highlighting the very human vagaries and passions that are almost always involved in learning and that may cause the student to turn a deaf ear to the call to educational adventure. Some of these strategies of resistance that students may consciously or unconsciously employ are to: (1) ignore the data, (2) reject the data, (3) exclude the data, (4) hold the data in abeyance, (5) reinterpret the data, and (6) change the old theory only peripherally. Because the types of resistance are so many, often so entrenched, and not infrequently politically motivated, Chinn and Brewer claimed that a person may *understand* a new paradigm—may even see its superiority—but still be able to rationalize rejecting it.

An alternative form of psychosocial resistance that students may consciously or unconsciously engage in to keep their psychosocial commitments intact is *strategic epistemic restructuring* (Vosniadou and Brewer 1987). This happens when students admit only enough conceptual change to mollify the teacher, but not enough to really modify their worldviews significantly. In other words, the student's strategy is to permit only "weak" conceptual change for the purposes of passing the test or just generally surviving the class, but to resist any "radical" change that would be truly transformative. In research into students' reading-comprehension, Dole, Niederhaus, and Hayes (1991) provided a large body of empirical evidence showing that students often "comprehend" a text (i.e., can perform well on tests), but do not actually "learn" from that text (i.e., do not experience durable conceptual change).

To be plausible and attractive to the student, then, the call to educational adventure and existential change must consist of a great deal more than just "tight" lesson plans, "correct" theories, or depersonalized teaching "methods"—the psychologically and culturally demeaning stuff that corporate schooling relies upon to ensure conformity in the student (and teacher). Rather, the student will respond—authentically, passionately, creatively—to the call to heroic education *only* if the teacher, out of the depths of *his* commitments, sagely and sensitively reaches out to the student in the depths of *her* commitments. The teacher must be alive to the fact that conceptual change problematizes the student's world and that she can not typically just give up old ideas and put on new as if she were trying on an article of clothing.

Considering John Steinbeck's novel *The Grapes of Wrath* as not simply a gripping story, but also an eloquent plea for socialism in America, entertaining the idea of parallel universes, or interpreting the attack on Pearl Harbor from the Japanese perspective—all of this may represent a very high-stakes existential game for a student, with serious consequences for how she communicates with her family, how she sees her culture and her place in it, how she imagines her future, and even how she conceives of and relates to the Divine.

Another way of putting this in strictly curricular terms is to say that just as there is (1) an "official curriculum" (usually mandated by a state, institution, or department) with essentially cognitive goals as well as (2) an "operational curriculum" (which refers to how a given teachers chooses to interpret and tailor that curriculum for her class), there is also (3) a "subjective curriculum" (Cohler 1989, 52. See also Eisner and Vallance 1985). The subjective curriculum refers to how the student *experiences* the official and operational curricula—what they *mean* to her in terms of their relevance to her life-world, how she *feels* about it all. The subjective curriculum includes "such factors as the [student's] relationship with both teachers and fellow classmates, the personal significance of the curriculum, and the importance of a sense of self as a requisite for taking on the challenge of new learning" (Cohler 1989, 57). As the psychiatrist Peter Blos wrote, in the early years of psychoanalytic interest in education,

> The past and present experiences of the individual will … determine his attitude to the subject-matter itself—the meaning it will have for him, his ability to accept it, and the purpose it will serve in his total development. What any [student] learns in a given classroom situation is an individual matter which can be understood only in terms of the experiences and attitudes he brings to it. No two [students] in the same classroom are having exactly the same experience. (1940, 492)

There are as many subjective curricula as there are students. Nor is the subjective curriculum limited to just the student's experiences. It also includes the teacher's experiences. Teachers also have psychological and cultural investments in what they choose (or are sometimes compelled) to teach (or not teach). Indeed, the subjective curriculum *must* involve the teacher's subjectivity because transformative education, relying upon authentic dialogue between teacher and student, is impossible without the subjectivity of both parties coming deeply in play. "Each one projects distillates of his own inner perceptions and experiences, past and present, onto the subject under study, be it mathematics, reading, history, or literature" (Field 1989, 853).

The idea of the subjective curriculum is a handy theoretical construct, for it helps to make sense out of an experience that most teachers have had many times—namely, that there may be two students of roughly equal intellectual ability who wind up performing quite differently throughout the term. Not infrequently, this is because the one student has a more robust "learning ego" (at least in certain fields or topics) than the other (Anthony 1989, 108). The learning ego (which is to say, one's level of confidence in oneself as a learner) is a sort of "horizon of expectation"—affected by conscious, subconscious, and unconscious factors—that a student has formed over the years about herself as a learner. This self-image will dramatically influence how she actually does or does not learn, for it is an educational truism that students with high self-esteem tend to learn better than those with low self-esteem. Math education offers a classic example of this aspect of the subjective curriculum that affected a very large group of students—females.

Female math anxiety (less prevalent now that in generations past, but still an issue in American education) was the sense of helplessness and dread that many women felt when confronted with a math problem. It was the result of a lifetime of explicit and implicit messages to women that they were incapable of doing well in math—and would be freaks if they somehow did manage to succeed. Not surprisingly, women tended as a consequence to do quite poorly in math. In the early years of the twentieth century, there were even scientists (some of them at such respected institutions as Harvard Medical School) who argued that the blood to the brain required for complex mathematical calculations would be diverted away from a woman's reproductive system while she did math; this would do irreparable harm to her ability to produce healthy children! (Tyack 1974). With the advent of feminist educational research and gender-sensitive pedagogies, however, women's math anxiety has been on the decline and their math proficiency on the rise over the last several decades. Their learning ego has been healthily bolstered by a psychologically sensitive and politically enlightened pedagogy, although there is still more to be done in this regard (Sadker and Sadker 2004; Tetreault 2001).

Depth psychology has provided curriculum theory with knowledge regarding "the many drive-determined aspects of learning—for example, conflict, anxiety, defense, repetition, regression, specific and nonspecific transferences and counter-transferences, and the like"

(Salzberger-Wittenberg 1989). These often undermine the teacher's best efforts, and this is why it is crucial that the teacher have at least a basic understanding of these phenomena (such as that provided in the preceding chapter) and how they may manifest themselves in students of all ages. Curriculum theory has, however, been slow to avail itself of these insights from depth psychology. Indeed, despite several important works on the psychodynamic factors involved in teaching and learning, an analysis of educational research over the last 80 years reveals that colleges of education have not attended nearly enough to the psychodynamics components of why a student may or may not respond to the call to educational adventure (Mayes, 2009). This is a situation that has to change. But it will only change if we as teachers and educational scholars pay more attention to the creation of what I have called "the therapeutic classroom" (Mayes 2007).

Before saying more about what I mean by a "therapeutic classroom," I would like to point out that I am not advocating for an overly permissive pedagogy that caters to the student's every emotional whim. I am not saying that a student should be coddled in old beliefs that do not seem to be serving her or others. I am simply noting that teachers must approach the attempt to encourage such sea-changes in a student's life in an emotionally adroit manner and with a healthy dose of realism about just how much the student's concepts *can* change in the course of just one term or even one year. A wise pedagogy attends to the fact that the student's emotional state affects her learning—just as her view of herself as a learner may affect her emotions.

The Therapeutic Classroom

Before getting into what I mean by a "therapeutic classroom," it will be useful to take a look at what psychiatrists who are interested in education have said about the relation between depth psychology and education since about 1920, when this research began. Fortunately (or unfortunately, as the case may be), this is not a difficult task since the body of literature on this topic is still relatively small. I have presented a review of the major statements and trends over the last eight decades in the field of depth psychology and education in my book *Inside Education: Depth Psychology in Teaching and Learning* (2007), as well as in my article "The Psychoanalytic View of Teaching and Learning: 1922–2003" (2009). Here I touch on only a few of those statements and trends to give the reader a sense of how the idea of the "therapeutic classroom" has evolved.

From the early years of research in the early 1920s into education and depth psychology, it was considered axiomatic that education and therapy, both requiring basic transformations in the ego, share a great deal of territory and therefore have many things that they can learn from each other. Oskar Pfister (1922) was a member of Freud's inner circle of disciples. He was a psychiatrist who, like Freud's psychoanalyst daughter Anna, began his career as a school teacher. Pfister pointed out that since teaching and learning are inevitably emotional processes, knowledge of emotional dynamics should be part of any teacher's professional preparation. Likewise, the psychiatrist Peter Blos contended that psychoanalytic knowledge should be a part of teacher education curricula in order to help teachers understand their students' general developmental issues as well as behaviors that might otherwise threaten, seduce, or confuse the teacher (1940, 505). In gaining and using this knowledge, the teacher is by no means performing some sort of "medical function" (Redl and Wattenberg 1951); however, it *is* part of the teacher's duty to help "relieve the child of some emotional pressure. At a minimum, it may keep him from getting worse. On the positive side, it may increase the probability of success in treatment being undertaken by outside agencies" (347)—a point that is even more relevant today than when it was made in 1951, owing to the much larger number of young people now in therapy.

Reflecting the political issues of many psychoanalytic educationists in the 1960s, Kubie declared that, because "the next goal of education is nothing less than the progressive freeing of man," the teacher could best reach this political goal "through psychoanalytically rich education" (1967, 70). Kubie's linkage of mental health and political health reflects a theme that one often finds in the writings of American psychiatrists since World War II, a time when democracy was being threatened around the world by totalitarian ideologies in Germany, Italy, Spain, and Japan—namely that a citizenry's emotional health is crucial to the maintenance of democracy. Neurotic people, it was felt, would not tend to make wise decisions, but would instead follow whoever played most craftily to their fears. With their focus on personal and political liberation, the 1960s and 1970s also witnessed insistent calls for the teacher to know "how to cultivate and deploy aroused imaginations, and their attendant emotions" in order to help free the child both intellectually and politically (Jones 1968, 85).

From the beginning of the dialogue between depth psychology and education, one of the most prominent themes has been that, although the teacher should perform a therapeutic function that is tailored to the unique context of the classroom, she should not try to be a therapist to her students. The psychoanalytic pedagogues even today generally continue to draw a clear line between therapy and education. At the same time, they are pressing for teachers to learn the basics of depth psychology and use simple common sense to create inviting learning environments. As one leading researcher in the field has put it:

> the teacher, if he or she is to be successful, must function as a psychotherapist, not in the formal sense of conducting therapy sessions with the students, but in the practical sense of being alert and responsive to the psychological needs that students evince both by what they do and what they do not do. (Basch 1989, 772)

For teachers who are afraid to consider psychodynamic issues in the classroom because they think that doing so implies that they are trying to be therapists, Field (1989) reminds them that it is the psychoanalytically savvy teacher who will know her limits and thus be *less*, not *more*, likely to try to perform functions that should belong to the therapist alone. Such a teacher will be well prepared in "understanding the barriers to learning, the unexpected hostility, so difficult to withstand, by which students [cover] over the shame of not knowing and the fear of failure" (Elson 1989, 805). Colleges of education have been quite slow to pick up on this point and include in their curricula any notice of such things—in no small measure because the corporate agendas for education that lour over schools also overshadow colleges of education (Valli 1993).

Still, the fact remains that the teacher's emotional and cultural insights and tact will be major determinants in deciding whether her students ultimately interpret her call to educational adventure as a threat or an opportunity. The depth psychological pedagogues have made it very clear that to have and exercise such tact in the classroom does not require a teacher to be a therapist. It asks only that the teacher be aware of the fact that deep things are going on in the student; that learning is a complex emotional affair; and that the teacher's gentleness, humor, compassion, and psychological savvy are indispensable in inviting the student to embark on the heroic educational journey. Shalem and Bensusan (1999) call this the "therapeutic conception" of teaching and contrast it with the traditional "mastery conception," which assumes that a student should be able to reject an old point of view and internalize a new one simply because the teacher presents "a better idea" or "good evidence"—or just because the teacher "says so." It views cognition as "cold." Now, better ideas and good evidence are critically important to education. Indeed, they are indispensable. By themselves, however, they often do not do the job if the ideas and evidence unduly threaten the student or are presented in an emotionally clumsy manner.

There are three ways that the "therapeutic conception" of teaching attempts to increase the likelihood that a student will enthusiastically respond to the call to educational adventure. First, it creates emotionally supportive classrooms where the student *wants* to be and is not merely *forced* to be. Second, it provides the teacher with a subtler understanding of learning, and thus renders the teacher more skillful in getting students to test and transcend their limits without pushing the students' limits so far that the whole enterprise goes up in the flames of reactionary resistance. Third, it helps the teacher guard her own emotional health (and thus be a more effective teacher) by providing her with the understanding that it is not necessarily *her* inadequacy that may be causing a student or group of students to be struggling with an idea under analysis in the classroom (although, of course, it may be), but the psychodynamic complexities inherent in the very nature of learning. In short, the teacher-therapist "is inclined to read [student resistance] from a perspective that recognizes that there are cases of ambivalence that actually reflect a state of internal conflict ... a condition in which the learner signals that she is undergoing a *process of change*" (Shalem and Bensusan 1999, 30).

This is why the teacher must be not only intellectually, but also emotionally adroit in relating to her students. She should be deeply reflective, too, regarding her *own* inner processes in the classroom. This means that she asks herself why she became a teacher, why she chose to teach the subject and age-group that she did, why she has decided to teach in certain ways and not others, and how being a teacher fits into the larger story of her life. In this manner, she begins to access her inner realms where psychospiritual processes impact her teaching just as her teaching experiences impact her psychospiritual processes. For this reason, I have frequently called for teachers to engage in "psychospiritual reflectivity," illustrating various ways of doing so (Mayes 1998; 1999; 2002a,b; 2005; 2007). Psychospiritual reflectivity by the teacher makes it more likely that the teacher's psychodynamic life will be as enriched by the heroic educational journey as the student's is. What is more, since the teacher who engages in psychospiritual reflectivity is much more in touch with her own inner life as it is going on in the classroom, she is able to be a better guide for her students, because she is teaching from a place of greater inner clarity. She is less likely to be a stumbling-block for her students, which can happen all too easily if her teaching is muddied by unresolved emotional issues about herself and her students.

A basic knowledge of depth psychology and a willingness to apply it to herself and her students in the heroic universe of the classroom—and to do so with common sense and humor—helps make a teacher not only more willing but also more able to create a therapeutic classroom.

ISSUES AND APPROACHES IN THE THERAPEUTIC CLASSROOM

Certain ideas from psychotherapy that were touched upon in the preceding chapter have proven especially important in the literature on education and depth psychology. This research has tended to feature one idea above all others: transference and counter-transference between the student and teacher are almost always present in the classroom—and can be healthy if understood and used well by the teacher, but damaging if not.

One of the earliest statements regarding the importance of transference in the classroom came from August Aichhorn (1925). He asserted that understanding transference would often be extremely helpful to the teacher in understanding why a student is responding to her in a way that simply does not make sense in terms of their actual encounters in class—and in extreme cases with either an enthusiasm bordering on idolatry or a discussion-deadening negativity. Aichhorn ventured the explanation that in some cases (and probably many cases) the student is transferring problems he has had with previous authority figures onto the teacher who is standing in front of him. "In such cases, what you see being enacted before your eyes are really only repetitions and new editions of very old conflicts of which you are the target, but not the cause" (1925, 88).

Drawing on her father's idea of "repetition compulsion," Anna Freud, educated as both a teacher and psychiatrist, elaborated on Aichhorn's observations by averring that "there is in the individual a compulsion to repeat in later life the pattern of his earlier love and hate, rebellion and submission, disloyalty and loyalty." She believed that because learning is such an intensely emotional experience, echoing over the student's entire psychological landscape, it is vital that the teacher understand that students will project some of their deepest fears and hopes onto a teacher, who may wind up looking like either a saint or an ogre to a certain student, and sometimes a saint during one class and a ogre during another one (Freud 1930, 109)! Negative transference onto the teacher seems to be a virtually inevitable consequence of the fact that any asymmetrical power relationship (as in those between a teacher and student, doctor and patient, employer and employee, foreman and worker) often stimulates negative transferences from the less empowered person onto the more empowered one. Redl and Wattenberg (1951) went so far as to claim that, next to the parent, the teacher is the most likely target of the student's projections—so large does a teacher loom in a student's life. This is why it is imperative the teacher know about the transference and its manifestations in the classroom.

Indeed, knowledge of transferential dynamics in the classroom—helping a teacher identify when she is the target of negative transference and know how to respond to it appropriately—can be key in preventing teacher burnout. When a student challenges her in a way that seems to go quite beyond the academic point being discussed in class and interrupts the respectful flow of classroom discourse, the therapeutically enlightened teacher understands full well that this "discursive noise" might be the result of the student's transference onto her—an emotional, not an intellectual, challenge. This knowledge aids the teacher in responding appropriately. It arms her with the insight necessary to build healthy emotional boundaries for herself—boundaries that will help her dodge the student's poisoned emotional darts. With such boundaries in place, the teacher is then more effectively positioned to politely but firmly deflect the student's negativity and discourage its reappearance. In short, knowledge of transferential dynamics prepares the teacher to take the moral high ground and respond wisely to those one or two students who seem to show up almost every term with an axe to grind against teachers.

The therapeutic teacher also knows that a student's transference onto her can be a positive thing to be cultivated, not a bad thing to be avoided. Peter Blos, an early leader in the psychoanalytic study of education, reminded teachers that they are often "safer" persons than are parents for a student to project onto. As Blos put it, the teacher "may be in a better position than the parent to help the adolescent deal with new emotions, and may receive the transferred feelings of the student as a parental figure" (Blos 1940, 494). In the 1960s, various scholars, noting the increasingly close connection between homes and schools, predicted that this would increase the propensity of the child to transfer family-of-origin issues onto schools and teachers (Grossman 1975). It may not be an exaggeration to claim that "once the transference is recognized, the teacher has the most powerful tool ever discovered to influence the lives of the students" (Kirman (1977, 49).

Again, however, it is crucial for the teacher to understand that she is necessarily walking a delicate line here as she attempts to be a therapeutically sensitive teacher, but not one who thinks she is her students' therapist. She is not. She does not need the intimate knowledge about her student that the student's therapist would, nor does she have a right to it. On the other hand, it is only common sense to recognize that teaching may have a healthily therapeutic dimension—and, indeed, must do so if the teacher is to be successful in her complex psychological task of encouraging the student to accept the call to intellectual adventure. Even a basic grasp of the psychodynamics of learning can be enormously beneficial for the teacher in showing her how to stimulate her students' instinct for psychological, intellectual, political, and ethical growth—and maintain it throughout the term.

In Kohut's terms presented in the previous chapter, we can see how easily and frequently teachers may receive the idealizing and mirroring projections of their students (Cozzarrelli and Silin 1989). The reader may recall that an idealizing transference is when Person A projects an ideal onto Person B, who then becomes an embodiment of that ideal for Person A. A mirroring transference occurs when Person A, feeling that her identity or some aspect of it is being celebrated by Person B, consolidates that part of her identity because Person B is affirming it for her. The teacher can use such transferences in order to model behavior that will make her a good "ego ideal" for the student.

Conversely, the teacher who does not understand the transference may unconsciously misuse its power to get her own ego-needs met at the expense of the student's legitimate need to find and emulate an ideal. This happens, for example, when a teacher tries to be her students' "buddy" to satisfy her desire, say, to be young again by being included in a fashionable clique of students. In doing this, she fails to provide her students with a stabilizing example of an emotionally mature and ethically responsible person who helps them think about complex issues in class. Becoming just "one of the gang," she fails to be an appropriate focus of her students' "idealizing projections." She relinquishes her claim to the archetypal role of Wise Elder—one that is so vital, as shown in the following chapter, to instilling the trust in the student that will allow him to embark on his heroic educational journey. Forfeiting this role renders the teacher unable to be a personal example of one who is sagacious and powerful—an individual in whom students, in a "mirroring projection," could see their own potential.

This example points to the larger issue that a teacher must also understand and control her own counter-transferences. When she does not do so, she runs the real risk of consciously or unconsciously using her students' idealizing transferences onto her as a way of manipulating them emotionally, intellectually, politically, or even sexually. Thus, it is very important that teachers reflect deeply on the psychological, political, and ethical factors that have played a role in both why they decided to become teachers and how they envision and enact "good teaching." In this way, teachers can root out what is problematic in their assumptions about teaching, modify what needs improvement or updating, and cultivate what is good.

In general, teachers are much more able to receive and positively channel their students' transferences onto them to the extent that they: (1) develop self-awareness, (2) seek satisfactions outside of the classroom, (3) evaluate possible dissatisfactions in their personal and professional lives and then seek help on specific questions, (4) talk things over with friends individually and in groups, (5) develop new avocations so as not to have all of their energy tied up in their students, and (6) recognize new possibilities in teaching so that the work itself provides emotional gratification that does not then have to be excessively garnered from relationships with students (Redl and Wattenberg 1951).

Whether she likes it or not, the teacher will almost always be some kind of Kohutian "selfobject" for a student, for "teaching ... is at least in part a selfobject function" in which the student discovers much of himself—his potentials and limitations—in his mirroring and idealizing transferences onto the teacher (Wolf 1989, 381)—further evidence of how deeply rooted learning is in the existential soil of the student's total emotional life. "Since our earliest learning arises in the intimate relationship of parent and child, each new course reawakens in students the need to have a target of idealization and to have their efforts admired" (Elson 1989, 789).

D. W. Winnicott's idea of a "holding environment," in which children can safely develop within acceptable boundaries of challenges, can be expanded to include the classroom as a challenging, but also safe, space in which the student can develop.

> Whether the course is biology, mathematics, sociology, or child care, the teacher provides a holding environment.... This holding environment is one in which the empathic un-

> derstanding of the teacher creates the conditions which allow the student to reveal what he does not know. Seeing the student at his least effectual, and yet nor breaking off contact or shaming him because of his limitations, becomes in itself a novel, healing experience for the student. (Elson 1989, 801)

As we saw above, in Winnicott's view it is not the "perfect" mother, but the "good-enough" mother who is most likely to create a realistic, sustainable holding environment for the child. Like the "good-enough mother," "the good-enough teacher" creates for the student a transitional space where he can experiment in ways that are both secure and challenging (Wool 1989, 750).

It is impossible to provide such intellectually dynamic, emotionally nuanced, and politically empowering education when, under the threat of the all-important high-stakes test at the end of the term, students live in fear throughout the term. This is why it is not only a pedagogical imperative, but a moral one that as teachers, researchers, parents, and citizens, we advocate for therapeutic classrooms—sacred educational spaces where the heroic teacher is able to issue the call to adventure clearly and fearlessly—and where heroic students have reason to hope that the educational journey lying before them will proceed with joy and in good faith.

CHAPTER 3

Entering the Perilous Forest

Responding to the call and crossing the first threshold as a process of death and rebirth

Of the many lessons that education can take from therapy, perhaps the most fundamental one comes from existentialist psychotherapy, the basic premise of which is that it is ultimately the fear of death that prevents a person from changing (May and Yalom 1995). I believe this fear of death often lies at the heart of a student's attempt to refuse to change her ideas about something—her refusal to answer the call to adventure by entering the "perilous forest" of academic adventure.

Indeed, it is easier to rest—however fitfully—in outmoded ideas and behaviors than to embrace the hard work of change. As many psychotherapists attest, getting a client to *understand* her neurosis is not the principal difficulty. The basic problem is convincing her to give up the neurosis, because an intellectual understanding of a problem is rarely enough to keep a client from persisting in dysfunctional behaviors or painful thought patterns. As shown in the previous chapter, and examined in more detail here, this paradox is equally prevalent in the classroom when a student, despite ample evidence and tactful persuasion to the contrary, still stays entrenched in an old idea that is patently false.

In therapy, the client's progress is often stymied by the fact that her problem is like a friend—a predictable part of her life, a source of certainty, as comfortable as an old teddy bear, falling apart at the seams but still good enough to snuggle up to at night. The same is often true of a student's outmoded concept or even worldview. This is why mere cognitive therapy is frequently as limited in its effectiveness in therapy as is the scientific model of conceptual change in the classroom. Just understanding something does not mean that we will accept it, even if it clearly represents growth and empowerment. Transformation requires the old to die so that the new may come forth. Hopefully, change will eventually bring the refreshing experience of renewal, but that comes later. The death must be suffered first—and, naturally, we instinctively recoil from that.

Death never comes with a guarantee of rebirth—only the *hope* of it—hope which (who knows?) in the last resort may prove to disappoint. The frightened soul asks itself: "What if I die to an old way only to find that no new way really emerges despite the therapist's or teacher's promise that it would? What if they are false prophets, their promises empty, and I am left with nothing but regret after they have worked their deceptive magic? Or what if the new way is simply unsatisfactory, proves to be something less than the people, practices, and places that I have promiscuously abandoned and now no longer deserve to have again in my life? Worst of all, what if the challenge to cross the threshold is merely a wicked invitation into quicksand? Having lost the innocence of my previous world, and being now trapped in a lethal world of muffled screams and sandy asphyxiation, what if I come to discover that I have given up psychological balance, cultural groundedness, intellectual certainty, and spiritual safety—only to perish beneath the surface of this pit I stupidly fell into?"

Learning is a leap of faith. The teacher must never underestimate what it may be costing the student in all sorts of ways to entertain a new worldview. The old ego and its ideas must allow themselves to be crucified, so to speak, so that more beautiful and powerful conceptual structures can form and a resurrected ego can arise. The mystery of losing oneself to find oneself lies at the heart of the hero's mythical journey—and the student's educational adventure.

This mysterious challenge is particularly insistent at the beginning of the Hero's Journey in many fairy-tales. There, the paramount problem for the initiate-hero is to find within himself the courage necessary to leave the sleepy security of his simple village-home, the warm embrace of his aging parents, and the tranquilizing certainties of his rustic country ways in order to cross that first threshold into the dark woods of adventure—rich in promise, but also in peril. The hero must summon up the courage to move out "just beyond the parental watch ... and beyond the protection of his society," where he had heretofore comfortably lived as a "member of the tribe"—one who has been "more than content ... even proud, to remain within the indicated bounds" (Campbell 1949, 77–78).

Ultimately, the question is this: "Can the ego put itself to death?" (Campbell 1949, 109). Can the individual cast off an old worldview, or at least elements of it, in order to enter "a new zone of experience," Jung's "sacred precinct," where emotional, moral, and intellectual transformation can occur? (Campbell 1949, 82). If so, then the hero and student, whether in the forest of adventure or in the discourse of the classroom, will come to know that "the crossing of the threshold is the first step into the sacred zone of the Universal Source" (Campbell 1949, 81).

EDUCATION FOR INDIVIDUATION: NURTURING THE EGO–SELF AXIS

The moment that one begins to press beyond the threshold of her ego, she begins to move into a sacred zone of experience and insight. Here, she transcends (but should never lose) her personal perspectives and inclinations. As consciousness begins "to go transpersonal" into a more universal, even cosmic, dimension—the gateway to which is the realm of the archetypes—it is vital that the changing ego still remain rooted in ordinary reality (Wilber 2000). As the old Buddhist aphorism reminds us, even the enlightened master must still "chop wood and carry water" every day. Going transpersonal should not obliterate the ego, for it is the ego that interprets and manages our everyday reality. The obliteration of the ego would mean the loss of one's grasp on the requirements of the workaday world, and the word for that is psychosis. A healthy process of going transpersonal, therefore, not only leaves the ego intact, but also refines it by providing it closer contact with the transforming spiritual wisdom of the Universal Source. The old ego, reenergized and restructured, emerges in a more mature and efficacious form. It becomes a more *spiritualized* ego.

This brings us to a paradox which mystics from all religious traditions have reported over the millennia—namely: the more one reaches *without* for the Divine, the more one finds it *within* oneself, at one's core. This psychospiritual core is what Jung called the Self, which "might equally well be called the 'God within us.' The beginnings of our whole psychic life seem to be inextricably rooted in this point, and all our highest and ultimate purposes seem to be striving towards it" (Jung 1953, 238). The Self is where the Eternal speaks to a human being in terms of both her deepest personal nature and her highest universal needs. It is her soul. As the psychospiritual "center" of the personality, the Self is the sun around which the planetary ego revolves in an eternally upward spiral of constant growth, what Goethe at the end of *Faust* called "eternal mind's eternal transformations." It is the Self, directing those transformations, that sponsors this ripening of the ego in insight and power.

Where the ego is in communion with the Self, then there exists what Jungians call an "ego-Self axis" (Edinger 1973). The lifelong cultivation of the ego-Self axis is the work of individuation. Connecting the practical world of the ego with the spiritual world of the Self, this axis allows a person to be more effective and more spiritual. Transformative pedagogy is primarily concerned with how educational processes can facilitate the development of this axis, which is why heroic education can also be called "education for individuation." Needless to say, accomplishing this goal requires authentic and profound engagement with the curriculum by the teacher and student. This is an emotionally, cognitively, and ethically demanding task. But nothing less will do if existential transformation is the goal.

In the heroic journey of individuation, the conceptual structures of ego-consciousness are constantly evolving through contact with the Divine. Likewise, in transformative education the student's ego is constantly maturing as she discovers facet after facet of herself and her destiny through the medium of the curriculum. This "education for ultimacy" is the alpha and omega of archetypal pedagogy (Huebner 1999).

EDUCATION FOR INDIVIDUATION VERSUS EDUCATION FOR NEUROSIS

Heroic education is *anti-neurotic.* It liberates the ego, fosters its communication with the Divine within, and suggests new vistas for the individual to explore and enfold into herself in her progression into ever richer experiences and expressions of her holistic being. How different this is from corporate education, which alienates a student from herself and is thus *neuroticizing*, forcing her to uncritically accept conventional "knowledge-structures" and official "facts" that may have outlived their purposes, may have never really had any coherent purpose in the first place, or (worst of all) may be serving someone else's subtle totalitarian program of psychological, political, and spiritual control. Corporate education carries on this toxic project by always holding over the student's head the threat of punishment and ridicule and the depressing prospect of academic and vocational failure. Conversely, it rewards students for assuming a pathological posture of timidity and impotence. Forcing the student into intellectual obedience in the classroom prepares her to be politically obedient later on. Indeed, it is hard to imagine anything that could better prepare students to passively comply with the demands of the totalitarian state than year after year of standardized instruction and assessment, as Richards has shown in his study of schooling in the Third Reich (Richards 2007).

Heroic education is education for democracy. It is constantly summoning the teacher and her students to think, feel, value, and act according to their most compelling ethical commitments and existential projects. A true democracy (unlike what passes for one in the United States today) requires education for individuation, for no democracy can be healthy if its citizens are psychologically unhealthy. Education for democracy celebrates curricula in which teachers and students freely explore themselves as political, cultural, and spiritual beings in a growth process. Only these pedagogical aims are consistent with the democratic ideal of the free individual in dynamic and responsible interaction with other free individuals. In the words of the psychoanalytic theorist Cornelius Castoriadis, democratic education consists in nurturing the student's "radical imagination and . . . the freeing of [her] capacity to make and do things, to form an open project for [her] life and . . . work with that project" (1994, 8).

Entering the Archetypal Classroom: Teachers and Students as "Subjects"

In responding to the call to educational adventure, the ego begins the process of transcending and restructuring itself by creating stronger ties to the Self, from which it can now receive greater measures of support and wisdom. This process—what Campbell (1949) calls the "millennial adventure of the soul"—is by its very nature an educational journey, and it can be happening anywhere, on any of the innumerable fields of experience: in a boardroom, meditation hall, or street corner; on a battlefield, mountain top, or football field. But the place that we explicitly privilege and set apart for the heroic educational journey is the classroom. Ideally, the classroom is what Jung called a *temenos,* a sacred space of deep personal and intellectual encounter and growth.

Although, as we have seen, the academic *temenos* houses a *community* of inquiry, the most important changes that occur in the classroom *temenos* are ultimately individual and profoundly interior, for what is being transformed is the student herself. The student-hero, like the mythological hero, "goes inward, to be born again" (Campbell 1949, 41). The teacher's job largely consists in helping the student make this inward turn in order to examine her present ideas in the light of newer ones, to ask herself if her old paradigms are still enriching her existence. If they are not, it allows her to "try on" the new perspectives being offered in the classroom.

This introverted, depth orientation is quite different from corporate pedagogies, which are *extraverted* and superficial. They wrench the student's gaze away from how something relates to her own intellectual, political, and moral depths, and force it outwards, towards a wasteland of mere data and sterile techniques. They compel the student to "learn" (which means to memorize) boring facts, empty procedures, and official theories (which are to be reproduced on the test). Explicitly and implicitly, students are flooded with the grim message (and more and more with each passing class, test, and year) that their joyless role in school, and indeed in life, is to acquiesce while they are evaluated by and then absorbed into various techno-corporate agencies and entities that make up the mechanisms of political and spiritual control in the brave new world of the twenty-first century.

In the last analysis, all of this is symptomatic of the fact that the American mentality is fixated on exteriority—obsessed with the production and consumption of goods, which Marx identified as the cancer of capitalism, what he called "commodity fetishism." Accordingly and increasingly, the function of U.S. schooling is to tear the student away from herself in order to turn her into a mere "producer" and "consumer" of goods and services. In Martin Buber's (1965) terms, depersonalized education turns existentially rich individuals, vibrant "subjects," into controlled "objects." Heroic education, in contrast, honors the student as a psychological, intellectual, and ethical subject who, through a vibrant "I-Thou" relationship with her teacher, is constantly giving birth to herself as an eternally evolving "subject."

The Archetypal Sanctity of the Teacher–Student Relationship

The archetypal nature of the relationship between the teacher and student is rooted in the fact that, from birth to death, we are involved in one ongoing educational act or other. Speaking of what he calls "the romance of the nursing couple," the child psychiatrist Winnicott (1992) has shown how infant and mother negotiate with and "teach"

each other about the delicate protocols of breastfeeding in the quiet intimacy of the feeding hour.[1] Every situation in which we find ourselves is potentially educative, depending upon how well we convey or discern its inner significance—its peculiar message to each of us as unique individuals, its broader meaning to us all as members of the human family. This is true at the end of the lifecycle no less than at the beginning. I remember every detail of the first time I saw someone pass on, for it was one of the most educative moments in my life. As my mother passed over with grace, humor, and faith, she acted (one last time) as my teacher, showing me how to die well—an example that I, as a good student, hope to emulate when my hour comes.

Teaching and learning, being universal and essential to the human experience in its most dramatic as well as its most ordinary moments, are archetypal by definition. To violate the fundamental sanctity of the archetypal teacher-student relationship is not only a pedagogical problem but, even worse, a moral one.

Let us look now at some of the basic manifestations of the archetype of the Teacher.

THE TEACHER AS A WISE ELDER

Since the heroic journey is essentially an educational process, it should come as no surprise that the first person whom the hero generally meets on his trek is a teacher. This teacher appears in the archetypal guise of the Wise Old Man or Wise Old Woman (often as an initiating priest, wizard, medicine man, or medicine woman), whose function is to guide the young initiate. Thus, the archetypal teacher's role is:

> precisely that of the Wise Old Man of the myths and fairy tales whose words assist the hero through the trials and terrors of the weird adventure. He is the one who appears and points to the magic shining sword that will kill the dragon-terror, tells of the waiting bride and the castle of many treasures, applies healing balm to the almost fatal wounds, and finally dismisses the conqueror, back into the world of normal life following the great adventure into the enchanted night. (Campbell 1949, 9–10)

This archetypal teacher may appear at various points along the journey as Obi Wan Kanobi does for Luke Skywalker in *Star Wars*. Or he may be a more or less constant presence for the hero as Virgil is for Dante in *The Divine Comedy*.

Research into the teacher's "sense of calling" supports the belief that many people become teachers because they want to fill this archetypal role of mentor in their students' existential journeys (Joseph and Burnaford 1994; Serow, Eaker, and Ciechalski 1992). Their primary motivations for taking on the complex and not especially lucrative job of teaching center around such impulses as their desire to foster their students' emotional health, promote their cognitive growth, develop their aesthetic sensitivity, and contribute to their ethical development. They wish to become teachers of "hope and promise" by helping students catch a higher vision of themselves, even when (and perhaps especially when) those students are in distressing and dangerous situations in life (Bullough 2001). They aim at helping the student negotiate some of the challenges of her existence.

I argued above for the necessity of creating therapeutic classrooms because of the distress that many students are experiencing in our increasingly imperiled world. But creating therapeutic classrooms is also important to teachers because it corresponds to the reason that many of them became teachers in the first place, by providing a milieu in which teachers tend to be more satisfied, and thus more effective, in their work. This is the most promising way of addressing the epidemic of teacher burnout in the public schools—with about half of our teachers leaving the profession within five years of beginning in it (Anyon 2001). Many of these teachers leave, not primarily because of the low pay, but because their psychospiritual sense of calling is not being honored—and in fact is being assaulted on all sides—by the impersonality of corporate education. Teachers come to see quite quickly that they are being forced by the system into the role of mid-level classroom implementers of impersonal, upper-level agendas—agendas that have little if anything to do with why they became teachers. Refusing to play such a role, teachers simply quit.

My nearly three decades as a teacher and educational researcher have convinced me that teachers are generally quite amazing people. They are usually motivated by such laudable impulses as love of their subject, a sense of social purpose, a wish for increased emotional intimacy with their students, and the desire to see their students blossom intellectually, emotionally, and spiritually. But even such heroic people are not immune to the demoralizing effects of policies and pressures designed to strip the classroom of its humanity. The Jungian psychologist Irene de Castillejo's observations about the archetypal reason why some general practitioners are unhappy in their work are also relevant to teachers. General practitioners:

> have been vociferous about their unjust remuneration and inferior status in the medical hierarchy, but I have never heard them mention what is much more likely to be the fundamental nature of their unhappiness: that the *archetype of a healer* which has sustained and nourished them throughout the centuries has fallen from their shoulders leaving them as little cogs in the great machine of modern medical practice. It is not a greater share of the world's wealth they lack, but "mana." (de Castillejo 1973, 22 [emphasis in original])

In like manner, educators need to be able to reflect on themselves in terms of the *archetype of a Teacher—a Wise Elder.* They need to be given the time and resources to view and renew their purposes and practices in ways that produce *mana*—the psychospiritual lifeblood of teaching. For this reason, I believe it essential that teachers be allowed, even encouraged, to engage in what I have called "archetypal reflectivity" (Mayes 1998; 1999) to help them clarify their aims, hone their skills, deepen their commitment to the work, and enfold their lives as teachers into the larger narrative of their lives.

The "called teacher" (Stokes 1997) who engages in archetypal reflectivity is better able to resist lesser views of her role and picture herself as what she really is—"the one who appears and points to the magic shining sword," a classical archetypal symbol of increased intellectual and discriminative powers (Jung 1958). The shining sword embodies the meanings engendered by the classroom discourse. The archetypal teacher holds up this shining sword as a gift, for it truly belongs to everyone in this particular community of inquiry. It symbolizes the teacher's and students' intellectual growth—which, of course, never happens through coercion or seduction.

The teacher who is able to tap into the archetypal *mana* of her sacred role feels greater joy and potency in her work. The student also experiences joy and potency in coming to view himself not as a hapless stranger standing on the outskirts of significant intellectual life (the student's "dragon-terror" of inadequacy and marginalization) but as an important member of a community of inquiry in the classroom (Brown, Collins, and Duguid 1989). She might even feel empowered enough to imagine herself as a future member of a particular "community of experts" in a field or discipline (Bruner 1960). The teacher, in publicly and genuinely wrestling with complex issues with his class, is playing the role of the archetypal Wise Elder in humility, modeling for his students how to wield the sword with integrity. Such a teacher, through his invitation to each student to join the community of inquiry, "applies healing balm to the almost fatal wounds" that the student may have suffered elsewhere through exclusion or abuse (Bullough 2001). He engenders hope in his students, and hope is the heart of spirituality.

Teaching rooted in the teacher's archetypal understanding of himself as guide and also fellow-traveler is psychologically and politically liberating for both the teacher and his students (Freire 2001). Through the medium of the curriculum, the teacher has helped his students pursue more rewarding ways of seeing, being, and doing in the world. This is the mythical "castle of many treasures" that each student can now—because of her positive classroom experiences—lay claim to with a greater degree of confidence and conviction. Having thus enriched and enlarged his students' understanding not only of the subject-matter but of their lives, he "finally dismisses the conqueror [student], back into the world of normal life," where she becomes a better partner, parent, professional, and citizen—a spiritual work in progress.

The Elder's Shadow

It must be kept in mind that caution and humility are also in order regarding the teacher's identification with the archetype of the Wise Elder. Otherwise, what Jung called "inflation" occurs (Jung 1953). This happens when, instead of drawing judiciously upon an archetype's energy to enrich one's total personality, one attempts to artificially pump his ego up by excessively identifying with the archetype. Instead of cultivating an archetype, one attempts to colonize it.

The teacher who does not merely access the archetype of the Wise Elder, but tries to stake a self-aggrandizing claim to it has fallen into potentially disastrous inflation. The teacher's challenge in archetypal education is to responsibly use the archetype of the Wise Elder in the service of the class, not to abuse that archetype to support a power trip. Carefully absorbing the psychospiritual energy of the archetype ennobles and enlivens the teacher and his practice, enabling him to guide his students to higher ground, but being inflated by it may easily cause him to harm himself and his students.

Jungian psychologists often describe inflation as *being possessed by an archetype*. When thus possessed, the teacher forgets that even in a field where he has a certain degree of expertise, that expertise, however great, is necessarily limited. Advanced degrees, and even many years of research, do not confer omniscience upon a teacher. That is reserved for God alone. Teachers can err, and it is best to frankly acknowledge this to oneself and one's students when it happens, not hide behind a mask of intellectual infallibility (Craig 1994; Shaker 1992). Students also have valuable perspectives, rooted in their own rich experiences, which they bring with them to the classroom and which everyone else in the classroom would often do well to consider. If this were not true, then there would be no possibility of dialogue. For, classroom dialogue presupposes that the teacher's knowledge, though adequate to the task at hand, is not complete, and that the student's knowledge, though incomplete, is potentially valuable.

The teacher who fails to see this and, instead of drawing from the archetype of the Wise Old Man to improve his practice, excessively identifies with it, loses a healthy sense of his own limitations. He begins to see himself as a kind of intellectual god—although his students describe him behind his back as a dictator or just a jerk. Most of us have had teachers like this. Such inflation happens not only with teachers, but also with all sorts of professionals—judges, lawyers, police officers, athletes, politicians, physicians—who self-servingly identify with the prestige or glamour of their offices and sometimes act in unseemly ways because they feel "above" ordinary people, above the rules. Forgetting that their impressive-sounding titles and degrees do not eliminate their naked limitations as mortal beings, they transgress professional and ethical boundaries, injuring those who trusted them.

When titles and degrees are not used humbly in the service of others, but as a way of propping up a teacher's imperial ego, they only serve to cast a particularly ugly light on those very limitations he is trying to conceal. Reflecting on oneself and one's students in the universal terms provided by archetypal psychology is important because it grants a vision of both how great we are and how small we are. This gives rise to wisdom, humor, and compassion both in and out of the classroom, highlighting the fact that one's life as a teacher and one's life as an ethical being cannot be separated. An old German professor gracefully embodied this for me thirty-five years ago.

Professor Nagel introduced me to the beauty of German poetry in my junior year at the University of California, Irvine. Shuffling into class in a black suit that he always wore and that was much too big for his small frame, his improbable eyebrows bushing in cascades of white over the black rims of his thick spectacles, and holding a weather-beaten volume with flowery Gothic letters engraved in it, he looked like a learned gnome. He was much loved on campus, and getting into one of his classes was no easy matter. I particularly remember a lecture he gave one late afternoon on Rilke's poem "Archaic Torso of Apollo." As the windows turned rosy with dusk, Professor Nagel read this astonishing piece aloud to us in German and then led us on a fantastic voyage through its many mystical mazes. In one of the most inspired lectures I have ever heard, his German (it seemed to my untrained ear) was almost as lovely Rilke's. When he finished, we all sat in a hushed, shared recognition of some just-remembered spirit that had suddenly entered our little room in this rickety old building on the edge of campus.

In that silence, as we all listened to the second hand ticking off the last minute of the class, everyone hoped the hour would never end. Suddenly, rousing himself and rising from the old dark-oak desk on which he had been sitting, Professor Nagel stretched out his hand with the volume of Rilke in it—as if offering it to the whole class. Taking a very deep breath, he then proceeded to recite, one final time, the concluding words of the poem: "Du mußt dein Leben ändern" ("You must change your life"). "Ja ... Ja ..." he said to himself, turning slowly around and shuffling out the doorway into the evening, leaving us, his students, behind like leaves that were still registering the disappearing wind. After a minute or two, we also rose and exited the lonely little room—but carrying within us a new resolve to "change our lives" as Rilke, and Professor Nagel, had implored.

Here was a teacher who knew and drew upon the archetypal energy of the Wise Old Man, but never in a self-serving way. In approaching his task and text with humility and always for our edification, Professor Nagel attained before our very eyes a more intense understanding of Rilke—a more electric sense of communion with him. This he did in order to bring *us*, his students, closer to the poetry that had so deeply engraved itself upon his life and was now, in like manner, going to engrave itself upon our lives, too. Transporting us to the archetypal realm by what he saw, said, and did, Professor Nagel humbly took on something of the power of a prophet. Jung wrote:

> Whoever speaks in primordial images speaks with a thousand voices; he enthralls and overpowers, while at the same time he lifts the idea he is seeking to express out of the occasional and transitory into the realm of the ever-enduring. He transmutes our personal destiny into the destiny of mankind, and evokes in us all those beneficent forces that ever and anon have enabled humanity to find a refuge from every

> peril and to outlive the longest night. (Jung 1966, 82, par. 129)

By embodying the universal archetype of the teacher in his own distinct way, a teacher "transmutes our personal destiny into the destiny of mankind." He summons and displays the numinous power of the archetype to endow others with a sense of their own potency, not to showcase his own. By example and precept, he is the Wise Old Elder who—in those sacred places where the road of heroic adventure passes through the protected space of the classroom—guides the student-hero down the road of academic adventure to the destination of profound transformation.

THE TEACHER AS HERMES

Education is largely an ongoing exercise in interpretation. Standing before the teacher and student is a certain text, event, theory, or product. How may they best *understand* it?

The art and science of interpretation is called *hermeneutics.* A hermeneutic theory is concerned with how to determine what counts as a legitimate analysis of something. This is a complex philosophical undertaking, involving such areas of inquiry as epistemology, phenomenology, psychology, linguistics, cultural studies, aesthetics, and historiography. Developing a hermeneutic theory is clearly beyond this book's scope and my ability. However, it is necessary at this point to talk a bit about hermeneutics, so the following will hopefully serve in a rough and ready sort of way as a hermeneutic theory: the interpretation of any idea or product in the classroom is valid to the extent that it fosters the students' holistic maturation as critical, sensitive, and self-actualized beings in conversation with and in the service of others.

The word "hermeneutics" comes from the name of the Greek god Hermes. Now, Hermes is an interesting fellow. He is "genealogically" related to those many "supernatural helpers" who show up in fairy tales, myths, and legends from all times and places around the world —all of whom provide a hero who has just crossed the threshold with "the tutelage of the supernatural" throughout the rest of his journey. Without such teaching, the hero would be doomed to fail because of his immaturity, fears, and (often enough) arrogance (Campbell 1949, 72). Frequently, this divine teacher takes the form of a "wizard, hermit, shepherd, or smith who appears—to supply the amulets and advice the hero will require" for his adventure. Just how important

Hermes was to the Greeks is evident in the fact that he was venerated as "the master of ancient mysteries of initiation, and represented that coming-down of divine wisdom into the world which is represented also in the incarnation of divine saviors" (Campbell 1949, 73n). The archetype of Hermes is closely related to the archetype of the Teacher.

Hermes was also worshiped by the Greeks as the "god of limits." Thus, whenever a student reaches a limit that she feels compelled, for her own growth, to test, and possibly to cross, we have good reason to believe that Hermes-as-Teacher is not too far away, hidden in a bush, mist, or cloud, or sometimes standing in broad daylight, with a bent finger and broad smile, urging the intellectual adventurer on—to go past the limits of her previous interpretations. Just a few yards beyond the boundary of the country village and immediately past the gateway to the enchanted land, the Teacher-as-Hermes stands, greeting and engrossing the novice-hero with his divine wisdom, welcoming her into the numinous realm, and pointing her attention forward to the wonders and visions that await. In fulfilling his archetypal role as a Wise One, inviting the hero to leave the simple truths of her country home and beckoning her to cross the threshold of adventure, the teacher takes on the role of Hermes.

The more adroitly the teacher can healthily draw upon the archetypal energy of Hermes, the better he is at promoting the hermeneutic maturation of his students. This teacherly role and function is psychospiritually powerful, and, because it is, it underscores the importance of teachers reflecting on their power. Through such reflection, teachers will be more likely to tap their power in ways that further their students' growth. They will also be less likely to misuse their power as Hermes, the god of limits, in bewitching and seducing their students to cross intellectual, emotional, political, or even sexual lines that are healthy and should not be transgressed.

The need for the teacher to reflect upon his role as Hermes is all the more evident when we consider that the psychospiritual energy that emanates from the archetypally exciting teacher is a manifestation of libido. We saw in Chapter 2 that Freud defined libido much too narrowly as merely sexual energy. Jung offered a broader definition. "Libido for me," he wrote, "means psychic energy, which is equivalent to the intensity with which psychic contents are charged" (1953, 52n). When someone filling an archetypal role taps into the Universal Source of psychic energy in the collective unconscious, the "electricity" is bound to be of considerable "voltage"—and, like actual electricity, can be used either for good or ill. Like the therapist, the teacher must be aware of his archetypally electric role in order to deploy it in a healthy manner with his students. For, although Freud was too limited in his sexual definition of libido, there is no denying Freud's insight that libido almost always has a sexual component to it, even in its most spiritual forms, as anyone who has ever read the Old Testament's *Song of Solomon* knows, with its sensual imagery of God's relationship to Israel as that of a husband and wife consummating their love (Nielsen 2006).

Freud often warned that psychoanalysis must be carried on "in chastity." This is because seduction in any form, physical or mental, is the ultimate type of manipulation. It turns the other person into an object. This completely poisons the transformative educational relationship, which, above all else, must aim at maximizing the student's empowerment as a *subject*. No less than therapy, then, teaching must be carried on "in chastity," physically, emotionally, and intellectually. If it is not—if, that is, the teacher is using his role to hoodwink and seduce a student into a belief or practice that is unhealthy and maybe even unethical—then the teacher has turned his student into an object of his seduction.

To learn how to use his power with students in ways that serve them and never enslave them is thus an ongoing ethical exercise for the archetypally powerful teacher. In Kohut's terms, he must be a healthy object of the student's "idealizing transference." In Winnicott's terms, the classroom must be a "holding environment," where students feel safe enough to reveal and examine who they are in order to become all that they can be. This means that it is the teacher's responsibility to reflect deeply upon his practice so that he can, like Winnicott's "good-enough" parent, create a space where students have no need to fear that their teacher is—either physically, emotionally, or ideologically—a predator who takes perverse pleasure in leading those who trust him into error. The teacher must be aware of Hermes's shadow—and never cast it over his students.

THE TEACHER AS TRICKSTER

What the Victorian literary critic Matthew Arnold said of great poetry is also true of great education: it is a matter of "high seriousness." But this does not mean that great education must be devoid of laughter or grimly self-absorbed. To the contrary. Humorless classrooms are usually deadly because they take the pleasure out of learning. As Shakespeare knew in writing some of his most emotionally intense works, unrelenting high seriousness finally overwhelms an audience. There must be some comic relief from time to time! This is as true in the classroom as it is in the theater, and is, in fact, one of the many parallels between teaching and the performing arts (Sarason 1999).

Transformative education is an existential gamble. Nothing less than the most important elements of our lives are under analysis and, to a certain extent, up for grabs. Death and rebirth are at the heart of any transformative curriculum, which stimulates the questions: "How can I live as fully as possible? And how does that life impact what, if anything, awaits me on the other side of the experience of death?" "To be or not to be" is not just an issue that Hamlet discusses with himself. It is the basic issue in transformative education, which aims at cultivating in the student the "courage to be" (Tillich 1952)—that is, "to be" emotionally, intellectually, and interpersonally authentic in a universe that sometimes seems indifferent to us, that seems to offer us only death as the final reward.

Thus, when Hamlet jumps into the grave and finds his old friend Yorick's skull there, he is leaping as well into the central question that transformative education always poses: how, through what is being studied in the class, can teacher and student reach greater levels of clarity about some aspect of the human situation in such a way as to not succumb to despair, but move forward with hope that is vibrant, yet unsentimental? One way to accomplish this is through humor. Thus, the scene in which Hamlet handles his old friend Yorick's skull and faces the fact that the dank dungeon of the grave awaits us all, also includes some of Shakespeare's best humor in the character of the gravedigger. The gravedigger's earthy humor takes some of the sting out of the starkness of the grave, and ultimately helps the audience (if not Hamlet) feel that death, although the grimmest of realities, may also be a preface to something else, something good.

The student on the verge of the forest, desert, sea, or jungle of adventure senses that the trek will have no shortage of dangers, and it is awareness of these dangers that naturally causes her to resist the call to heroic education. Like Hamlet, she is, in a sense, jumping into a grave, where elements of her old identity will be buried. Throughout the student's educational odyssey, the teacher's humor will play an important role, just as the gravedigger's does for Hamlet, in helping her see the lighter and more hopeful side of it all. The teacher's humor at the beginning of a term is his way of signaling to the student that, despite the enormity of the task that lies before them both, there is every prospect that things will turn out well. It sends the message that despite the challenges that await both teacher and student during their shared ordeal of existential exploration, there will be plenty of opportunities along the way to rest, enjoy each other's company, and even bask in moments of recognition and mutual affirmation.

At my university, I teach the graduate seminars in multicultural education. There is no field more complex or contentious than that of multiculturalism. There is even a body of literature that has arisen around the best ways to teach this potentially explosive subject. Multicultural issues pose the most serious sorts of challenges to both students and teachers regarding some of their most impassioned beliefs about themselves and others. From birth to death, every individual is embedded in at least several cultures and subcultures, and in the complex conditions of the postmodern world sometimes many more than just several of them. Many of our beliefs arise out of and are constrained by cultural factors, and none of our beliefs are ever totally free from them. To begin to analyze (and usually this means to problematize) one's own and others' culturally rooted beliefs and identity is rarely anything other than an emotionally charged, discursively risky, and philosophically challenging endeavor. If ever humor were needed in a class, my class on "Educating Diverse Populations" *is* that class!

I generally take a two-pronged approach at the beginning of the term. On one hand, I make it clear that multicultural education is a matter of high seriousness. Issues of the broadest world-historical import as well as some of the most intimate personally significance will be involved. Nor (I emphasize) are these just theoretical matters. The views we, as educational leaders, ultimately adopt regarding multiculturalism in our society will impact many students' lives in fundamental ways—and, if our choices are not wise and humane, our decisions and practices will impact those lives in destructive ways. These are not laughing matters.

Yet, on the other hand, at the end of the first class, I usually perform my famous "ear imitations." I am proud of the fact that my ear imitations have gained such notoriety around our college of education that many students whom I have never met before come to the first class expecting to see them—and ask me why I did not do them on those rare occasions when I forget. These imitations include my rendering of such notable sets of ears as those of Mr. Spock, George W. Bush, Barack Obama, Evander Holyfield, Vincent van Gogh, and (that sure-fire crowd pleaser!) Elmer Fudd imitating Dumbo, with his flapping ears singing "I Believe I Can Fly." My grandmother was a vaudeville comedienne in the Jewish theater in the early 1900s. My mother grew up in that environment, loved it, and soaked it deep into her being. I hardly remember an hour throughout my entire youth when mom would go without falling into a truly hilarious routine or string of one-liners. She often entertained dad and me with her mock ballets (once she lost her balance during one of them and went pirouetting off through a rickety wall in our living room), and almost every evening she did a fan-dance with the plates as she was putting them on the table. Mom was simply the funniest person I have ever known. So I suppose that I was genetically predetermined to do such things as ear imitations—not to mention my also justly celebrated "Jimmy Does Jimi" series, in which I imitate Jimmy Stewart singing the music of Jimi Hendrix.

Naturally, the classes love this. It humanizes me as a teacher and it makes the subject-matter more approachable to them. It is proof to my students that I meant what I said at the outset of class—namely that, despite my years of multicultural study and experience, and despite the fact that one of the texts we will be studying is one that I wrote, I do not pretend to have a monopoly on the truth regarding multicultural issues for the simple reason that no one does. "These are supremely complex topics that we will all be wrestling with throughout the term, and perhaps some of the most complex issues you will ever encounter as a student, teacher, or principal," I tell them. Being flat-out goofy with my students, letting them laugh good-naturedly at my (very willing!) expense assures them that although I take my responsibility of teaching multicultural theory seriously, I try not to take myself all that seriously.

In a way, this humor is like a down-payment on my promise to my students that I will always remain open to their critiques of my views (as long as those critiques are polite), that I will always offer any critiques of their views in a similarly constructive and civil manner, and that we all must work hard to forge a constructive dialogue around these hot-button issues—one that is frank but never sarcastic or abusive. Humor is the indispensable ingredient in making this potentially explosive class into one of the students' favorites, judging by the fact that it generally gets some of the highest evaluations of any class offered in my college of education.

Through humor, the teacher encourages the student to withdraw some of her excessively idealizing transferences onto the teacher. Humor creates a "safe space" for the student, a "holding environment," where she feels both secure and empowered enough to grow. It also assures the student that the teacher is not perfect (and that, therefore, the student does not have to be perfect either in order to succeed or gain love!) but that the teacher is, in Winnicott's terms, "good enough" to guide her natural, steady development. This good-natured, creative, and inviting energy—which does not distract from the high seriousness of the subject but, like the gravedigger's humor, paradoxically allows the teacher and students to see their subject and each other more clearly—is available in any class where the teacher can judiciously tap into and adroitly embody the archetype of the Trickster. In this way, the teacher completes the invitation to the student to enter the forest of academic adventure called the classroom.

NOTE

1. Ekstein has noted that "the first curriculum struggle ever developed does not take place in school but rather ensues between mother and infant as she is nursing her baby. The full breast is the first curriculum the baby must empty and digest in order to meet the goal and requirement of satiation" (1969, 49).

CHAPTER 4

Initiations, Tests, and the Wise Elder

Having left his village, heard and accepted the call to adventure, and committed himself to the journey, the hero now: (1) undergoes an initiation, (2) sets off down the road of trials, (3) after awhile approaches and enters a cave, castle, or some other type of enchanted dwelling, which is symbolic of an encounter with the archetypal Great Mother, and (4) encounters a paternal figure, symbolic of the Great Father. In this chapter, we examine each of these stages of the journey in order to discover what they can tell us about the archetypal nature of teaching and learning.

Becoming a Member of a Community of Discourse in the Classroom

"Initiation is a rite of passage ceremony marking entrance or acceptance into a group or society. . . . In an extended sense it can also signify a transformation in which the initiate is 'reborn' into a new role" (http://en.wikipedia.org/wiki/Initiation). What "group" or "society" is the student entering in the transformative classroom? What is the "new role" into which she is being "reborn" at this stage of the heroic adventure?

To answer these questions requires that we look first at a theory of knowledge and approach to education that has been consistently gaining ground since the 1980s: social constructivism. This school of thought rests largely upon the work of Lev Vygotsky, a Soviet psychologist of the early twentieth century. Social constructivists believe that all knowledge is socially created, and that this fact has wide-ranging educational implications. The social constructivist's pedagogical goal is to turn her classroom into a lively "community of inquiry," one that is infused with interpersonal interactions where the student—under the guidance of the teacher—works with his fellow students to formulate questions and generate answers in the social construction of knowledge in the classroom.

As a Marxist whose emphasis as a psychologist was on the social nature of human awareness, Vygotsky (1986) claimed that it is wrong to look at consciousness as something that exists all by itself, in a social vacuum. We discover, use, and create knowledge, he argued, in interaction with other human beings. Vygotsky was not simply asserting that every individual's consciousness is affected by social circumstances—something that we would all probably agree to. His claim was much more radical than that. He insisted that the individual's consciousness is not merely *influenced* but is actually *produced* by the social situations in which she finds herself from birth to death.

The so-called "individual" (which in Vygotsky's view is more a theoretical construct than an ontological reality) is a sort of "node" in the total social network. She is a bundle of sensations, emotions, beliefs, expectations, and cognitions that has been formed and is constantly being re-formed by a specific interplay of social forces at this particular point in social time and social space. Vygotsky saw the "individual" as embedded in concentric rings of social realities that completely determine who she is. The social environment comes first; "individual" consciousness comes second, as merely a specific byproduct of the social environment. Consciousness is awareness *of* a social situation; it is also awareness produced *by* that situation, all of which means that consciousness can never exist *apart* from the social situation which engendered it. Social constructivists therefore say that all knowledge is "socially mediated."

We get a more concrete sense of these theoretical assumptions in social constructivism by looking at how it views the all-important phenomenon of memory. Memory is one of the most important manifestations of consciousness because whatever an individual is thinking at this very moment is ultimately just the most recent "edition" of the stream of consciousness that has been flowing, virtually without pause, throughout her entire life. The present is, paradoxically, just the most recent expression of the past. Even if something entirely new to a person enters her field of consciousness at a particular instant, she will necessarily be seeing and interpreting it in reference to and in terms of things she was conscious of before—in both her recent and more distant past.

Now, just as memory is the core of thought, so "situations and events" (and according to the social constructivists, all situations and events are either explicitly or implicitly social) are at the core of memory. Vygotsky offers a delightful example of this:

> If you ask a child to tell you what a snail is, he will say that it is little, it slithers, and it sticks out its foot; if you ask him to tell you what a grandmother is, he is likely to reply, "She has a soft lap." In both cases, the child gives a very clear summary of the impressions which the topic has made upon him and which he recollects. The content of the thinking act in the child when defining such concepts is determined not so much by the logical structures of the concept itself as by the child's concrete recollections. It is syncretic in character and reflects the fact that the child's thinking depends first of all on his memory. (1986, 50)

The core of thinking is memory, and the core of memory is those situations in which the person has found herself throughout her life. Think of a concept as simple as "policeman." For an upper-class white child whose neighborhood is carefully guarded by polite and helpful policemen, this concept will evoke a very different set of associations than it will for an African American child from the ghettoes of Detroit, where the child and her family may have experienced policemen as aggressive, disrespectful, and untrustworthy for many years, even for generations. The word "policeman" is the same for both children only in the most superficial sense of how it appears on a printed page. What it actually *means* to each child is radically different, and this difference is socially mediated. But, it might be objected, even granting the premise that concepts arise from the memory of particular situations and will, therefore, always be colored by the nature of that situation, are all situations necessarily "social"? How about concepts that someone learns in situations where she is alone? Aren't such concepts simply a matter of individual cognition without reference to any social factors? "No," reply the social constructivists, and their reason lies in the nature of language.

Social constructivism relies heavily on the Sapir–Whorf hypothesis in linguistics. This hypothesis has two prongs. The first is the assumption that individual consciousness is formed by the terms, categories, and points of view available in the language of her specific culture. The second is that languages vary a great deal from each other in how they allow a person to interpret reality. Vygotsky and the social constructivists have turned to sociolinguistics to strengthen their claim that consciousness is fundamentally social. In particular, systemic linguistics has been most helpful in showing how consciousness is socially formed in children, for it is felt that if we can understand the foundations of consciousness in childhood, we will be able to understand it better in its more complex forms in adulthood.

The research of sociolinguists M. K. Halliday and Basil Bernstein, the fathers of systemic linguistics, has offered great insight over the last several decades into the sociolinguistic foundations of the child's consciousness and what all of this means to the educational enterprise (see Forbes 2003). Systemic linguistics insists that the child learns who she is by learning about herself in the various social situations in which she is constantly finding itself—something that almost always involves the learning of her culture's language(s). Indeed, she learns not just the language, but rather a specific *form* of it that is used in the stratum of her society in which she is "positioned." Her dialect of the language may possess quickly identifiable differences from the prestigious dialect of that language that is spoken by the people in power in her society—differences in such things as pronunciation, vocabulary items, grammatical constructions, and rhetorical patterns. Her dialect thus identifies her not only as a member of a general "culture," but also as a member of a particular "subculture." If she learns the dialect of the socially dominant classes, that language will then provide her with a great deal of "cultural capital." If her dialect comes from a socially marginalized group, it will provide her with very little "cultural capital" (Bourdieu 1977).[1] But whether the dialect spoken is prestigious or non-prestigious,

> as the child learns his speech ... he learns the requirements of his social structure. From this point of view, every time the child speaks or listens, the social structure of which he is a part is reinforced in him and his social identity is constrained. The social structure becomes the child's psychological reality by the shaping of his acts of speech. (Bernstein 1971, 124)

Social constructivism turns the popular belief that "thought creates language" on its head, postulating instead that it is social situations that create and convey language, which is what makes thought possible. Vygotsky (1986) therefore rejected the Swiss psychologist Piaget's idea (very popular in many educational circles in the 1960s and 1970s) that thinking was essentially an individual affair—and that there were "cognitive structures" somewhere in the brain that were both prior to and independent of the social origins of language.

Now, to return to the woman sitting in a room by herself who is having an original thought: Isn't that an example of consciousness as a purely individual phenomenon going on independently of any social influences? Not at all, said Vygotsky, because for that woman to be thinking anything at all, she *must* be speaking to herself (even if silently) in order to formulate her thoughts, for thought is simply internalized speech.

To see what Vygotsky means by this, try to think a thought without internally saying any words. It is impossible! Thus, even if you were sitting alone in the depths of the remotest reaches of the most obscure jungle in the world, hundred of miles from any human being, you would still be engaged in a social act every time you had a thought, because you would necessarily be using language, which is a social tool—indeed, the quintessential social tool. Consider this, too: when you are speaking, you must be speaking to someone. Who is it? If it is not someone whom you are actually addressing at that moment, then it must be to an imagined person or group of persons who make up the implied "audience" of your internal declarations. In that jungle, you are still involved in a conversation with others every time you think a thought.

In making such bold claims that all human thoughts and experiences are necessarily social, I feel that the social constructivists have —despite the many important insights and humane practices that they have introduced in educational practices—taken the "individual nature versus external influences" debate too far in the direction of "external influences." To be sure, we, as social creatures, are profoundly affected in many ways by our social circumstances. However, as individual children of God engaged in a process of eternal evolution, each one of us is also more than just the sum of the physical and social effects that have impinged upon us in this brief lifetime. The individual's soul, her "Self" (in Jungian terms), exists before and goes on after its "tour of duty" in this dimension of being—or so I believe.

But this book is not a theological study. It is an inquiry into the nature of teaching and learning. And from that vantage point, social constructivism has been a great boon to education, giving rise to many fruitful and exciting ideas and practices over the last several decades. These have all served to help many educators cultivate the potential of the classroom to be a community of inquiry, a brotherhood and sisterhood of intellectual and ethical exploration, a communal place where the student is initiated into a fellowship of joint exploration and creation with her classmates.

Even if learning is not *exclusively* a social act, it is without doubt *largely* a social act. And as a matter of fact, most of us seem to learn best when we learn with others in a supportive environment. We tend to solve problems more creatively when we join our skills to those of others. As many people intuitively know, and as most teachers understand through years of experience, successful educational environments are generally built upon "socially shared intellectual work, and they are organized around joint accomplishment of tasks" (Resnick 1987, 18). It is into this community of learning that the student-hero is to be *initiated* as a new member, largely through the actions of the skillful teacher.

In an influential essay written by Brown, Collins, and Duguid, the authors noted that "situations might be said to co-produce knowledge through activity" (1989, 32). In other words, "knowledge" is not just generalized and context-free awareness of "facts"—the staple of standardized testing. Doubtless, such decontextualized "knowledge" serves certain limited and mostly technical functions. This is not, however, what learning should be about—and certainly not heroic learning. For, "activity and situations are integral to cognition and learning. . . . [B]y ignoring the situated nature of cognition, education defeats its own goal of providing useable, robust knowledge" (32). To learn in a vital, enduring way, in other words, is not to learn sterile abstractions or mere bits of information that do not meaningfully relate to the teacher's and students' actual lives as physical, emotional, intellectual, cultural, and ethical beings. Rather, education should be about jointly encountering, as a community of discourse, questions and tasks that are vitally related to the actual situations in which teachers and students really *live*, both in the classroom and in life. This was the credo of the liberal wing of the American progressive educational movement in the first half of the twentieth century and is still the guiding notion in student-centered pedagogies (Cremin 1964).

This brings us to one of Vygotsky's most important ideas for education—and one that highlights the role of the student as someone who is either being initiated into an area of inquiry or as someone who is initiating another student. This is his idea of the Zone of Proximal Development, the notion that cognitive growth is "development as determined through problem solving under adult guidance or *in collaboration with more capable peers*" (cited in Wertsch 1985, 67–68, emphasis added). This means that if Student A knows more about something than Student B, Student A may help Student B learn that thing, because Student B is still close enough to Student A to learn from her: the two students are *proximate* to each other's *zone of development* regarding a particular idea or skill. Student A is thus able to initiate Student B into a new community of discourse (or into a new aspect of a community of discourse in which they are already jointly engaged).

The lovely thing about cooperative pedagogies is that at some point during the term, Student B is bound to know more about a certain topic or task than Student A does. This allows the two students to switch roles so that now the person who was previously the initiator is the one being initiated, and vice versa, creating a sense of mutual assistance and joint empowerment. This allows the teacher to avoid those unnecessary and hurtful forms of cut-throat competition in the corporate classroom that destroy the humane spirit of heroic education. Cooperative learning also furthers the cause of heroic education by fostering practices that allow students and teachers to engage in education that they find relevant to their existences.

BECOMING A COGNITIVE APPRENTICE

As the teacher draws students together in a class, she initiates them as members of a community of discourse. But there is yet another way that the teacher, like the archetypal Wise Old Man or Woman, initiates her students. This is an initiation into a far larger community of heroic inquirers than just the small one in the classroom. As the teacher increasingly familiarizes her student with the questions that actually concern "experts" in a particular field, and as she shows her students (often by modeling it for them) how experts go about dealing with these questions, she is in effect urging her students on to become "cognitive apprentices" in that field.

Students become informally but authentically *initiated* into a professional community of discourse that extends far beyond the classroom and may even encompass the whole world—particularly with the growth of the worldwide web. By initiating a student into a larger community of inquiry, the teacher may well be helping a student take a significant first step down the road of actually becoming an official member of a certain professional community of discourse—whether that community is made of up artists or engineers, poets or athletes, parents or entrepreneurs.

Pedagogies that encourage cognitive apprenticeships solve a large problem in education—namely, the disparity between what students learn in a classroom and the way that practitioners in a field actually think and operate (Schön 1987). This is the famous disconnect between theory and practice.

> Unfortunately, students are too often asked to use the tools of a discipline without being able to adopt its culture. To learn to use tools as practitioners use them, a student, like

> an apprentice, must enter that community and its culture. (Resnick 1987, 33)

In education as initiation, the teacher can be pictured as a master "cognitive artisan," a Wise Elder, teaching his cognitive-apprentices how to inquire and create as people in various professions and disciplines do. This current trend in instructional theory stems from Jerome Bruner's famous structure-of-the-discipline theory, where the teacher, by both explicit instruction and implicit modeling, shows students how to handle problems in a given field by learning how "experts" in that field do their work—but always, Bruner adds, in ways that are developmentally appropriate to the child's present stage. The "structure of knowledge" in a discipline must thus form the pedagogical basis for the "structure of instruction and learning." In his work in the 1960s, Bruner explained how the structure of almost any discipline could be tailored to the capabilities of almost any age group. Bruner explained:

> Any idea or problem or body of knowledge can be presented in a form simple enough so that any particular learner can understand it in a recognizable form. The structure of any domain of knowledge may be characterized in three ways, each affecting the ability of any learner to master it: the *mode of representation* in which it is put, its *economy,* and its effective *power*. (Bruner 1960, 44)

Bruner admitted that, of course, "mode, economy, and effective power vary in relation to different ages, to different 'styles' among learners, and to different subject matters," but he insisted that each of these three aspects of the structure of a discipline could be adapted to students' knowledge and abilities at virtually any point in their development.

Bruner's famous anthropology curriculum, *Man: A Course of Study*, attempted to translate this theory of curriculum into practice. In this curriculum, students were not simply taught facts about anthropology. They were guided in how to think like anthropologists do. The specific form of such curricula will naturally vary according to the histories, world-views, and objectives of the specific discipline, the students' stage of development, and the inclinations and objectives of the teacher. But whether the subject matter of the curriculum is physics or literature, psychodynamics or auto mechanics, the way experts in the field approach their work should be the way students are taught to approach it. In this manner, the teacher as Wise Elder initiates his novice-heroes into academic adventure and points them down a road that may take them exciting places in life, long after the class has ended.

An especially meaningful example of this comes from the life of my niece Cristina. Cristina was basically majoring in partying during her first two years of college—a "field" in which she was excelling because of her stunning beauty and magnetic charm. It was not clear to others and me that she would ever actually get a bachelor's degree. Even assuming she did, it was anybody's guess what in the world she might major in since she had shown no particular interest in anything. Then she took an introductory biology course from Professor Davidson.

This professor's passion for biology captivated Cristina, who suddenly discovered that she was not only interested in the subject, but good at it, too. Professor Davidson, recognizing Cristina's aptitude, allowed her to be his lab assistant. Although her tasks were necessarily quite simple at first, he used them as an occasion for introducing her, step by step, to the actual issues in biology that were the focus of his research—and always in a way that was suited to her stage of development at any particular time. According to Cristina, Professor Davidson, by treating her as a sort of apprentice-biologist (who was, in her own smaller, but still authentic ways, engaging the same issues that her professor was), enabled her to catch a vision of herself as someone who, through patient commitment and hard work, could someday be a master-biologist, too.

That "someday" came very soon. In less than two years, Cristina had completed all the work for a biology degree and had even traveled with Professor Davidson to Tokyo to present a paper at a prestigious international conference as one of his co-researchers. The next year she was accepted at the University of Colorado Medical School. Three years later she received an M.D. with honors as one of the top students in the class, nabbing a very desirable internship in anesthesiology. From party-animal to doctor of medicine in five years!

To be sure, Cristina has inherent gifts that allowed her to do this marvelous thing. But they are gifts that may have remained dormant for a very long time had it not been for a professor who, as a master-biologist, a Wise Scientific Elder, treated his student as an apprentice-biologist, thereby propelling her down a road of academic adventure. It is an adventure that has resulted, for my heroic niece, in intellectual and emotional growth, professional empowerment, and a lifetime of opportunities to be of service to others.

Down the Road of Tests and Trials

As William Blake, the English Romantic poet, wrote, "Without opposition there is no progression." This is a basic fact of human existence, for without challenges to meet and overcome, the individual would have no need to grow. Indeed, without challenges, the individual would have no *way* to grow, for most change happens as a way of dealing with some felt inadequacies in the present. This is why in my faith tradition Eve is not vilified as the originator of sin but honored as "our glorious mother Eve" (*Doctrine and Covenants* 138: 39). She was the first human being to recognize the most crucial fact about transformation—namely, that it cannot take place without trials and tension. Without conflict, Eve understood, humankind would simply luxuriate forever in a sleepy paradise of static innocence, strolling eternally and aimlessly in a physically lush but morally barren garden because it could not offer its inhabitants any opportunities for growth. Adam's legalistic lack of imagination was (thankfully!) trumped by Eve's more penetrating intuitive awareness of the need to be tested.

For similar reasons, occasional testing is also necessary in the heroic academic journey. However, from the early grades to graduate school, the way testing is generally carried out in American education too often serves no constructive purpose—and does not contribute to the student's emotional, intellectual, or ethical growth. Rather, tests are too frequently designed to "monitor"—in an act of pedagogical "surveillance"—how well the student has memorized and can reproduce the "official" facts and received theories that make up curricula devoid of imagination and critique. Such testing not only fails to reflect a student's maturation as a member of a community of discourse; it actually prevents her from developing knowledge of or love for the spirit of inquiry that actually exists in such community. Often enough, such forms of testing kill any interest that the student might have already had or potentially developed in the subject.

Authentic versus Inauthentic Assessment

The standardized tests that are coming to dominate the landscape of educational assessment can do emotional, cognitive, political, and spiritual damage to a student because:

> those personal qualities that we hold dear—resilience and courage in the face of stress, a sense of craft in our work, a commitment to justice and caring in our social relation-

> ships, a dedication to advancing the public good in our communal life—are exceedingly difficult to assess. . . . [W]e are apt to measure what we can, and eventually come to value what is measured over what is left unmeasured. . . . In neither academic nor popular discourse about schools does one find nowadays much reference to important human qualities. . . . The language of academic achievement tests has become the primary rhetoric of schooling. (Rothstein 2000, 418)

This is not to say that students should not be tested. A student will scarcely grow if she can simply rest content in the illusion that she knows enough already and has no reason to change. However, testing should be *authentic*. Authentic assessment (a phrase that is central to humane educational theory and practice) refers to those lively and even enjoyable forms of evaluation that help a student gain a personally significant and academically productive sense of how much she has progressed. When testing is authentic, it also can suggest to a student which new directions to take for further growth. How different this is from the typical kinds of tests that students must confront throughout their academic lives! Such traditional forms of testing are generally unhealthy because they are *static* and *punitive*.

Traditional forms of testing tend to be static because they merely measure a student's knowledge (fleeting, because she will probably forget it as soon as the test is over) of an inert body of facts or an official series of theories. This fosters inert conformity and militates against robust creativity. Such testing modalities are also punitive. "How many did you get wrong?" is a question that students typically ask each other when they receive their scores on a test. In other words, how expertly was the teacher able to trap you in not knowing an "ideal" body of knowledge that has been defined by unseen authorities for reasons that often have little, if anything, to do with the subtle multidimensionality of a student's "understanding" of subject and even less to do with a student's "degree of intelligence"? Even such an apparently positive student statement as "I got 91 percent on the essay exam" also means that that student fell about "one-eleventh" short of a "perfect" understanding of the issues that the essay question revolved around.

Even more damning to testing that is designed to monitor and quantify the student's deficits, is the emotional wreckage that such testing leaves in its wake. The last several decades of educational research have shown beyond any possibility of controversy just how psychologically injurious, even fatal, it can be to the student's "learning ego" and sense of self-efficacy for her to fail such a test (Anthony 1989). This damage is even more unacceptable when we consider that failure on traditional forms of testing is often due to the insensitivity of such tests to a student's differential learning style, emotional issues, cultural perspectives, linguistic limitations regarding the language of the test, restricted life-chances for gaining the cultural capital necessary to score well on the test, or even what she ate (or did not have enough money to eat) for breakfast before going to school.[2]

In many ways, succeeding on such tests is even more damaging to a student than failing. Success on such tests may foster in a student the illusion that she now knows all she needs to know about something because she has received the magic grade of "A"—that ultimate educational narcotic. Such "positive" reinforcement too often deadens the student's desire for further inquiry and critique. It also sends the self-contradictory message to students that they are personally loveable and valuable to the extent that they score well on ultimately impersonal instruments of assessment.

Although there is an enormous body of research demonstrating the psychosocial harm that failing on such tests engenders, there is very little written about the psychosocial harm that succeeding on such tests also creates. If scoring well buys a student affection and approval, the hidden message "on the flipside" (and one that she cannot fail to register) is that *not* scoring well on such tests will result in withdrawal of affection and approbation—and that, indeed, she is an "important" and "good" person (indeed, one who is "more important" and "better" than students whose numbers are lower than hers) to the extent that—and only so long as!—she continues to score well.

This toxic consequence for the student of receiving these messages from teachers, parents, and the media is the creation of deep-seated performance-anxieties and aggressive impulses to constantly compare herself with others. These psychopathologies stunt her existential growth as a fearless, dynamic, creative, and responsible being who loves knowledge and delights in using it in the service of others. As Ekstein and Motto (1969) warned, such testing leads to students who have been emotionally blackmailed into submitting to the inauthentic project of "learning for love." This is absolutely contrary to the "love of learning"—both the process and the goal of transformative education.

Authentic assessment, on the other hand, nurtures a student's commitment to a lifetime (and possibly an eternity) of learning. It does this by permitting the student to see, in terms that are meaningful and growthful to her, just how far her understanding of something has developed through the emotionally nurturing and intellectually stimulating experiences she has had in class. And, because authentic assessment is existentially rich and interpretively open-ended, it also suggests new avenues of inquiry and action for the student to pursue after the test and term are over. Assessment then serves to celebrate the fact that the student's engagement with a subject has grown in personally relevant ways. But it should also be designed to gently yet clearly help her see that she does not know enough already, and indeed never will know enough, since any educational journey, to qualify as heroic, involves ongoing growth in knowledge and empowerment. Perhaps this is what Dewey meant in his famous statement that "the only cure for education is more education"(1916). There are many ways to test a student authentically (Dorn, Stanley, and Madeja 2004; Janesick 2006; Keefe and Jenkins 2008; Mezeske and Mezeske 2007). I do not wish to review that literature here. What I would like to do, however, is offer two examples of authentic assessment from my own practice.

One way in which I try to assess students authentically is to set my students a broadly summative question at the end of the term, one which requires each student to make holistic sense—in terms that matter to her because they are meaningful to her and indeed come from her—of all that we have read and discussed throughout the term. For instance, in my seminar in multicultural theory, I often ask students to address the following question in their final exam:

> Drawing upon our readings and conversations during this term, how has your view of the increasingly multicultural nature of American society and education changed, not changed, or changed in some respects and not others, from the view you held at the beginning of the term? What in our readings, discussions, and your private processing of these issues has resulted in the similarities and/or differences between your initial views and your current ones?
>
> Note that by "private processing" I am not only referring to your strictly "academic" engagement with these issues but also to how your emotional responses, ethico-spiritual evaluations of what has happened in class, discussions with significant others who are not members of the class, and other personal experiences both before and while taking this

class, have figured into how and why your views have or have not changed this term.

This kind of end-of-the-term assessment allows, indeed requires, a student to interpret the *whole* term *holistically*. Students have two weeks to write this essay. The only "length requirement" is that the paper be long enough to say what the student feels needs to be said in order to answer the question to the student's own satisfaction. It is due the next to the last class meeting. During this class, students divide into groups of three. Each student presents her paper, as if at a scholarly conference, to the two other members of her group. It is the task of the two auditors in each group to offer responses to the paper and suggestions for further research. The presenter then has two weeks to revise the paper if she wishes and turn it in the week after class ended. I then write my comments on the paper and return it to her. She then has one more week in which to make further revisions if she likes, allowing me time to read it once more before posting her grade for the term—a grade which, as discussed below, she gives herself.

Another form of authentic assessment that I employ is to encourage students to create an artistic product—a poem, song, sculpture, or painting—that captures their perspective on multicultural education. I emphasize that this should be a serious piece of art in the sense that the student should not simply dash it off one evening in half an hour, but should think deeply about it, which may involve something like keeping a journal leading up to the first act of creation and continuing until she has finished the piece of art—and maybe even beyond. During the last class of the term, students who have gone this route present their piece and then respond to the class' questions and comments about the piece of art. My students have created some quite remarkable pieces but, to me, the most moving one was created in my curriculum theory seminar.

In this class, I had a student whom I will call Dave. Dave was a graduate of West Point, a captain in the Army who had just returned from a tour of duty in Iraq. Between that tour of duty and a second compulsory tour that was coming up the following year, Dave was pursuing a master's degree in education. For his final "exam" in my curriculum theory seminar, he decided to do a series of watercolors—alternately playful and serious—each of which portrayed one of the seven aspects of the holistic curriculum as presented in my book *Seven Curricular Landscapes: An Approach to the Holistic Curriculum* (2003a), which we read during the term. The seven watercolors expressed his evolving understanding of the idea of a "curriculum."

We held our end-of-term class-party at his house. About halfway through the evening, his wife took me aside. She quietly told me that Dave had spent many hours, late into several nights, working on the project, which was, she said with a smile, obviously very different from any other task he had been set as a West Point cadet or as a tank commander in Iraq. I like to think that it was, in some measure, what he discovered not only about curriculum theory, but about himself in this heartfelt exercise in authentic assessment that led him, a few weeks later, to do the professionally very unwise thing of asking for a transfer out of the prestigious Armored Division (where his military career would be assured and might even result in him becoming a General in the future) to the marginal Division of Civilian Affairs (belonging to which would not only slow down his advance up the ranks, but would prevent him—for political reasons in the Army—from ever advancing above the rank of Lieutenant Colonel). Although professionally disastrous, this turned out to be a supremely healthy move for Dave and his family. After finishing his final tour of duty in Iraq (where he would be much more out of harm's way in his new role), he planned to leave the military, do a doctorate in education, and open his own school for at-risk kids.

I do not pretend that his final project for our curriculum theory class was the sole reason that he made such momentous—and, in my view, heroic—decisions about his life. There are certainly many deep and complex reasons for this sea-change in Dave, one which ultimately had a wide variety of constructive consequences in his personal, family, and spiritual life. But I believe that one of those reasons was the experience he had in a transformative educational setting which, by nurturing his heroic academic journey, contributed to his broader heroic journey as a noble man of intensely patriotic, ethical, and spiritual commitments, which he now felt would be better served as a principal of a school than as a tank commander.

I allow students to grade themselves both on all class work and for their final grade. After receiving extensive oral and written comments from me on their work throughout the term, they see that this way of assessing is not just a ruse on my part to sidestep my responsibility to respond to their work. I make it clear that I am "giving away" the political power of holding grades over their heads throughout the term for a reason and the reason is this: no matter how charming a song I might sing about wanting to draw my students into a shared adventure of discovery throughout the term, I would, in fact, be proving the song false, limiting their agency and circumscribing their creativity, if I maintained ultimate power in the classroom by holding on to all the academic capital in the form of grades. "There is no such thing," I point out to them, reminding them of Paulo Freire's important insight, "as a dictatorial pedagogy of liberation. You cannot force people to be free or use that freedom well. You can only invite them to do so. So this is my invitation to you. And it is now up to you to decide how you will respond to it and use your freedom."

As risky and counterintuitive as it may seem to teachers to let students grade themselves, I have found that in most cases students do so with a rigor and honesty that amply justifies my fundamental belief that when offered a genuine call to educational adventure—a call originates in the teacher's respect and love for her students' existential complexity, moral agency, and eternal potential—most students gladly and gratefully rise to the challenge of becoming all that they can be for themselves and for others.

THE "DEEP TEST"

Different teachers find different ways of assessing students authentically. The only limit to the types and scope of authentic testing is the teacher's and students' imaginations. Each teacher will find the approach or mix of approaches that best suits her and her class from term to term. What should not vary, however, is the teacher's commitment to what I call the "deep test," which should always be going on for teacher and students alike in the course of a term.

The deep test consists of an ongoing series of questions throughout the term: "Am I engaging with the readings, lectures, and discussions in class in good faith—which is to say, as honestly and intensely as I am realistically capable of doing, given my own talents and challenges, as well as the other legitimate commitments and constraints in my life? Given that I am engaging the curriculum in good faith, how is my knowledge of the issues under analysis in class becoming more subtle and humane? Even more importantly, how are these changes aiding me in my growth in (at least some of) the holistic domains of my life as a physical, emotional, intellectual, political, cultural, and ethical being? In what ways can I use this growth as an occasion for building a more creative and hopeful life-narrative for myself and others? And, moreover, what am I learning in this class that contributes to my development as a potentially divine being in an eternal process of ever-expanding creativity and goodness?"

The teacher's most fundamental role, I believe, is to help students internalize the deep test so that it will become a permanent fixture of their lives—one that will continue to operate within them even after the term ends, one that will permeate many aspects of their being. How can the teacher accomplish this? An answer to this question lies in the realm of archetypes—and in a return to an ancient Western pedagogical tradition.

SOCRATES AS TRICKSTER

We have already looked at how the teacher dons the archetypal mask of the Trickster as a clown in order to humanize himself and the educational adventure in the eyes of the student, allowing the student to feel safer in crossing the threshold and beginning the journey. Humor makes the archetypal power inherent in the role of teacher less daunting for the student. Being less forbidding to the student, but still maintaining his essential archetypal power, the teacher is thus in a better position to be of service to the student.

The Trickster also serves more complex functions for the student on the road of academic adventure that runs through the frequently tangled jungles of deep inquiry. Although Trickster is often funny, he is more than that. He is often irritating. Not infrequently his behavior is scandalous. And from time to time, he is even a little dangerous. The jokes he tells, the masks he wears, and the tricks he plays can be quite disruptive socially. Yet, this disruptiveness is ultimately healthy because it is intended to make his audience look critically at popularly held beliefs that need examining. This is why Trickster, through his playful, sometimes mischievous pranks, turns socially accepted definitions of normalcy and reality on their head.

We see this in Shakespeare's play, *King Lear*. King Lear's Fool "entertains" the king with a steady stream of absurd antics, intractable paradoxes, and brash challenges to the dignity of the king's person. If it were anyone else doing this, of course, the king would have that person's head swiftly removed from him. How come the Fool gets away with such things? It is because the Fool's humor, irony, and occasional effrontery do not come from a place of anger—and are certainly not meant to hurt the king. Rather, they stem from the Fool's poignant love for his befuddled monarch. They are meant to jolt his master out of his stupor and into awareness—into a realistic appreciation of just how dangerously limited the king's current view of things is, how potentially fatal his decision to give away his power to his two treacherous daughters, and, in general, how precarious his grasp on reality.

In modern societies, it is typically the comedian who plays the Trickster, using scathing and even scandalous humor to jolt society out of its collective stupor and thereby awaken it to its inadequacies and injustices. In short, the comedian often plays the fool *for* us, and even plays tricks *on* us, but all of this he ultimately he does in our service. His intent is to force us to grow beyond the easy (and therefore often dangerous) half-truths of our social conventions and see things more truly in all of their historical relativity, conceptual ambiguity, and moral complexity.

The classic example of the Teacher as a Trickster in the Western tradition is Socrates, as Plato portrays him in his *Dialogues*. Socrates's *modus operandi* is well known, of course. He shows up at a gathering and there either begins a conversation or breaks into one already in progress. In this conversation there is inevitably someone, and usually various people, throwing around a term or concept of great significance with reckless abandon: justice, truth, love, reason, courage, beauty, God.

Playing the role of a rather bumbling old fellow who knows very little, if anything, about the theme of the speaker's discourse, Socrates begins to ask him a few questions, which Socrates claims to be posing so that the speaker will clarify for him, poor old stupid Socrates, just what he, the very clever speaker, means when he uses the concept *A*. "Well!" the speaker usually replies to Socrates, often with some degree of condescending impatience, "By *A* I simply mean what everyone means when they say *A*." "Please tell me, then—an old nitwit who does not know what everyone else knows—what you and they mean by *A*?" With this, Socrates has very cunningly set the bait and the speaker has taken it. This is where the fun begins. For Socrates now starts to unravel the speaker's "understanding" of the concept *A* like the fluffy ball of mixed-up yarn that it actually is. Or, rather, Socrates lets the *speaker* unravel it himself through his own increasingly inadequate answers to Socrates' increasingly searching questions.

"But wait just a moment! If you mean such and such by *A*," Socrates muses with feigned puzzlement, "then wouldn't it have to follow from that definition of *A* that Proposition *B* must also be also true? But clearly you can't mean that Proposition *B* is also true, for it certainly seems manifestly false to me!" "*B* is certainly not true!" the speaker instantly replies. "You're right there, Socrates!" "Well," Socrates then sadly observes, "it seems as though you had better redefine *A*, hadn't you, so that it doesn't lead to *B*? Oh, and while you're at it," adds Socrates, almost as an afterthought, "I suppose you ought to make sure that your new definition of *A* also includes Proposition *C*, which, I assume that you, like me, *do* believe to be true, and which does seem to follow pretty clearly from *A*." "Indeed I *do* believe Proposition *C* is true and Proposition *B* is false. Thanks for pointing those things out, Socrates. So here—" announces the once again self-satisfied speaker, quite convinced that *now* he has reworked definition *A* so that it can overcome any other possible challenges, "here is my new and improved proposition!" And with a triumphal flourish, the speaker declares, "Behold! I give you … Proposition A_1! Surely that will satisfy you, Socrates!"

"Very good, indeed!" Socrates agrees. "You have cleverly restated *A* in such a way that it is consistent with both the truth of *C* and the falseness of *B*. Well done! I wish I had your facility with thought and were not just the old blockhead that I am." "Nothing to it, Socrates," is the speaker's magnanimous reply, "for if I do say so myself, you are right in observing that I'm really very good at this kind of thing." "I'll say you are!" Socrates seems to concur. But just as the speaker is about to go on with a new series of grandiose proclamations to anyone who cares to listen to his new round of bombast about A_1, Socrates rather deferentially breaks in with a new line of questioning.

"Hold on for just one moment, would you, please, Sir? I really don't mean to be a bother—you know me, I'm always so confused about the simplest things—but something else just popped into my brain that I am hopeful (given how well you answered my previous questions!) you'll be able to explain to me in just a few words." "Let me hear the question, my dear old fellow," the speaker, fortified by his recent victory, magnanimously proclaims, "and I'll get it cleared up for you in no time flat!" "Well, that's a relief!" Socrates will then say with a sigh of gratitude, concealing the fact that he is beginning to move in for the kill.

"You said," Socrates observes, "that A_1 being true, makes room for the fact that *B* is false and *C* is true." "Exactly right, Socrates! That is precisely what I did, in fact, say—and I have to admit to a sneaking admiration of my own brilliance in accommodating all of those propositions in one grand definition. Pretty amazing, really! Sometimes I surprise even myself." "Amazing, indeed!" Socrates concedes, and goes on: "Still, I just can't seem to get this one more pesky thought out of my brain, and that is this: If *B* is false and *C* is true, then I imagine that there is no way around the conclusion that *D* must also be true." With this, the speaker's face changes in a second from triumph to despair. For, as Socrates then observes, "Any child knows that *D* is false, so false that no man in his right mind would ever even begin to claim that it is true. If he did, we should consider him a lunatic, would we not?" Deflated, the speaker realizes that A_1 has landed him in as much hot water as *A* did. "Yes, we would consider him mad, Socrates. I guess that neither my original understanding of *A* nor my amendment of it to A_1 really work, do they?"

"No, they don't," Socrates says. "A_1 is every bit as flawed as *A*—and in some ways, even more so. I really thought that you had nailed it with A_1 but now we come to see that A_1 is as faulty as *A* was. What ever shall we do about this? Would you care to venture a new proposition A_2?" The chastened speaker, realizing that he has reached his wit's end, humbly confesses, "No, I don't, Socrates, for I can see that, despite my previous confidence, I really have no idea in the world what I'm talking about!"

Before the reader's very eyes, the speaker's smug confidence in his "understanding" of something has changed into a frank admission that he really does not understand it—and, indeed, may not ultimately not know much about anything at all! With the hammer of his questions, Socrates has broken down the flimsy structure of the speaker's opinions, revealing them to be a flimsy mass of contradictions, improbabilities, and prejudices. Throwing up his hands in despair, realizing that he no longer has any firm foundation upon which to stand, the speaker comes to realize that the only thing he knows about *A* is that he knows nothing about it, which he now admits.

"Excellent!" proclaims Socrates, now with genuine enthusiasm and even a touch of admiration for the man, "for *that* is where all true wisdom begins: in the admission of our serious conceptual limitations—even our ignorance! For, we human beings ultimately know just one thing for sure, and that is that *we know nothing for sure*. Now that we've stripped you of your naive certainties (which, in the final analysis, turned out to be quite indefensible and—let's face it—not a little dangerous in their reckless arrogance!) let us together, in a spirit of cooperation and humility, get down to the business of trying to maturely approach this issue like adults. We shall now inquire into this issue not on the rickety basis of what we think we know, but rather from the realistic recognition of our fallibility."

"And we shall be able to approach issue *A* freshly now, and with some modest hope for limited success," Socrates goes on, "because we will be aware at every step of our journey that we will probably never understand this—or any other issue—fully. Complete understanding is for God alone. And so let us agree in our discussions about this issue to always honor its complexity. This will enable us to pursue our academic adventure in a truly heroic fashion—that is, with increasing compassion, authenticity, and faith. In this way, we shall attain the true goal of education, which is not to be clever, but to become wise."

In my own teaching, this is the approach that I—in my own imperfect way—try to emulate. That is, I try to help students see the enormous complexity of things. "No one has a monopoly on the truth," I state in the very first class meeting, "and this includes me. True, I've read a lot more on these issues than you have, and I've undoubtedly given them a good deal more thought than you have, but my views (although more informed than yours at this point) are also incomplete. I, too, am always growing in my understanding of the history of American education. In light of our discussions and readings this term, some of my views may change as well—especially because most of you are public school teachers with many years of rich field experience that I lack, but which I can benefit from."

I then present the syllabus, in which I briefly discuss the core features of various approaches to the history of American education (Traditionalist, Revisionist, Postmodern, neo-Liberal, neo-Conservative, and Functionalist). I point out that there are strengths and weaknesses in each position, yet I also disclose the fact that I generally find that the Revisionist and Postmodern analyses of American education are the most useful. I then go on to emphasize the passage in the syllabus where I state: "There are other perspectives as well that we will examine in the course of the term. One of your major tasks in this class will be to begin to identify which theory, theories, or combined aspects of various theories are most compelling to you in terms of your personal experiences, pedagogical practices, cultural perspectives, ideological leanings, and ethical commitments. Let me stress that *I encourage you to take whatever positions you feel are most fruitful*. Indeed, one of the major purposes of the class is to show that there is validity in a great range of opinions (from the very conservative to the very radical) about American education and that *no one has a monopoly on the truth*. Hence, *in discussions, in the essay, and in the final paper, agreeing with my positions will not gain you a higher grade, nor will disagreeing with me get you a lower one*. Indeed, it is to eliminate such possibilities that I ask you to grade yourself for individual assignments and for the final evaluation. What is more, my position on these issues (as on most issues) is itself always a work in progress. I therefore not only allow, but genuinely look forward to the expression of diverse opinions on these complex matters. Since we will discuss a variety of controversial issues, the only requirement in class is that we all show the proper respect for each other's ideas and conduct our conversations courteously."

Student evaluations of this class show that my students usually feel that I accomplish these goals. I believe this is the case for several reasons. First, students see me genuinely wrestling—in front of class—with difficult issues about which I can form some educated first-hits, but not definitive solutions. Second, they see me authentically attempting to honor as many viable opinions about an issue as possible, even attempting to synthesize them when doing so seems good, and politely deconstructing certain opinions and perspectives that, in my considered judgment, simply do not work.

Third, they repeatedly hear me invoke my motto throughout the term whenever (as is often the case) we are face-to-face with an issue of truly daunting complexity. The motto goes like this:

> It is very often the case that any "answer" you or I may propose for a certain problem will "buy" us some advantages in dealing with that problem, but will also "buy" us some limitations in dealing with that problem—and may very well generate a new set of problems to boot! Our goal is not to find the "perfect" answer to a problem. Very rarely does such a thing exist in this ragged old world, where ambiguity and so many legitimate yet conflicting interests abound. We often will not even be able to find an answer that can confidently be called "the best" among our range of options. What is "best" for one of you, in your particular educational and professional contexts, may not be the "best" for the others. But here is what we reasonably can and ethically must aim at: to form answers (provisional ones because always subject to revision) that promote our own and others' physical, emotional, intellectual, political, and spiritual growth as fellow-travelers on the road through mortality.

In this way, the classroom becomes a site of humane inquiry, a zone of epistemological adventure, and a garden of ethical fruition. In short, it becomes a heroic adventure in transformation.

The Socratic Trickster-Teacher who teaches in humility and humor, and with a real passion to advance his students' heroic journey, will find that it is not only they who are evolving, but him as well. In transforming others, the teacher is himself being transformed in his own quest down the dialectical road of heroic inquiry. In this way, the classroom under the guidance of the Trickster-Teacher becomes a site of high seriousness as well as humor—and all are edified and built up in an ongoing act of pedagogical nurturance. Indeed, above all else in a class, there must be good-natured laughter punctuating every hour

—laughter at one's inevitable inadequacies as a mortal being in the messy process of grappling with the intractable paradoxes that lie at the heart of our existence, and which constitute the ongoing Deep Tests of our lives. And here is precisely where the miracle of transformative education lies: in confronting the contradictions and complexities that riddle our lives at almost every step, we, both as teachers and as students, grow in intellectual, emotional, and ethical power as we travel together down the road of academic adventure and spiritual growth.

NOTES

1. This is why the form of the language that a child speaks serves to identify her at a school-site as a member of such-and-such a group (primarily ethnic and socioeconomic) and, in so doing, either opens up or closes down educational opportunities for her regardless of her inherent talents or intelligence (Bernstein 1996; Halliday 1975; Rogoff 2003).

2. There is a vast body of literature on the inadequacies and injustices involved in standardized testing. For the reader who wishes to look into this more deeply, the following list of references provides a good place to start: Anyon 2001; Bernstein 1996; Bowles and Gintis 1976; Brophy 1994; Deyhle 1986; Ferdman 1990; Garcia 2001; Gardner 1983; Gonzalez 2001; Heath 1983; Jones, Jones, and Hargrove 2003; Kaulback 1989; Kozol 1991; Mayes, Cutri, Montero, and Rogers 2007; Oakes 2000; Ogbu 1987; Pepper 1989; Tetreault 2001; Tharp 1989.

CHAPTER 5

The Great Mother, the Great Father, and the Reward

Having heard the call to adventure, left his country village, crossed the threshold, and met his guide, the hero is now prepared for two pivotal encounters. The first is with a woman who embodies the archetypal energy of the Great Mother. The second is with a man who represents the archetypal energy of the Great Father. These two shaping experiences will prepare the hero for the Supreme Ordeal—the culminating test. If he passes this test, his heroic status is assured. Endued with vision and power, he can now return to his society to revitalize it. This completes the Hero's Journey.

Who are the Great Mother and Father? What does the hero's encounter with them tell us about the archetypal nature of transformative education?

THE GREAT MOTHER

In Taoist philosophy, the Great Mother is known as Yin, the eternally feminine principle of the cosmos—receptive, fertile, nurturing. She is the "ground" of existence both literally and figuratively (hence the etymological relationship between the words "matter" and "mater"). She dynamically absorbs energy and transmutes it into new manifestations of life. Topologically, she is associated with intuition and feeling. Grasping things holistically as a unified field, she operates through intuitive bolts of insight that are emotionally satisfying and morally compelling. As we saw in Chapter 3, the occasional shifts in scientific worldviews that constitute a "scientific revolution" typically occur when a "paradigm shift" takes place, when someone breaks out of the box of a particular worldview to ask a wholly new question—one that emerges out of a radically new intuition about the basic contexts and eternal tendencies of things (Kuhn 1970). This is the one of the activities of the Great Mother. It is her intuition that opens the door to scientific revelations.

Every cosmology—that is, model of the universe—is a "figurative language ... a new symbol for that same enigma which confronted all ages before us" (Jacobi 1974, 118). Every cosmological model—as a structure made up of symbols that reveal certain aspects of existence but occlude others—buys us some things, but costs us some things as well. A product of the Great Father, the Enlightenment cosmology of the eighteenth century portrays the universe as a machine made up of basically lifeless matter that organizes itself according to universal mathematical laws. This model has bought us all the wonders of science. But it has bought us all of the terrors of science, too. It has also functioned in Western culture to strip the universe of the sense of mystery and meaning that invest human life with significance and hope.

On the other hand, maternal cosmologies—which inform a great many Native American cultures—allow teachers and healers a variety of more poetic symbol-systems of the universe, which, although they have not resulted in jet engines or antibiotics, enhance practitioners' efficacy and satisfaction in their work. This may explain the growing interest in First Nation spirituality, medicine, and psychology among the technologically advanced countries. Securely rooted in the prolific soil of the Great Mother, First Nation cosmologies provide an important balance to those of the Great Father. I have seen the importance of the Great Mother in my work as both a teacher and counselor.

THE GREAT MOTHER'S MAGICAL MYSTERY TOUR

Several years ago, I was counseling a young man who was a methamphetamine addict. We had a powerful first session and bonded immediately. Since he was in crisis when we met, we spoke mostly of some crisis-management techniques he could use until our next session, when we would start getting more deeply into the story of his life and addiction. Outside of telling me that he had been adopted as a small child, he shared no other personal details of his life. We set up an appointment for two days later. The next night, before our appointment the following day, I dreamed of being in a room and looking through a sliding glass door. I see a drug deal going down next door. I decide to make a list of the license plate numbers of those involved and turn it into the police. A few hours after I woke up from this dream, my client, Steve, knocked on my office door. It was time for his appointment.

As he sat down, the first words that came out of his mouth were, "Cliff, after our session, I felt better. So I got online and, for the first time, really tried to track my birth-parents down. I found my mom after just a couple of hours of looking. I asked her about my dad. I had heard some rumors over the years that he had been heavy into buying and using drugs and had committed suicide. But do you know what my mom told me? She said that although my dad had been involved in drugs for a long time, in his mid-thirties he decided to turn over a new leaf. He stopped dealing and using. And Mom told me that he became so "anti-drugs" that he would take down the license plate numbers of drug dealers and turn them into the police. And that's how he died. Some dealers that he had done business with before found out what he was doing, and they killed him. He didn't commit suicide at all! He was murdered because he was doing the right thing! He got off drugs and fought against them. He was a hero, not a loser!"

This was liberating knowledge for Steve. It turned out to be the first big step on his road to recovery. In the dream, I had been given an advance glimpse of information that would help him resolve a crucial issue. Like certain other teachers and counselors, I occasionally experience precognitive dreams and synchronicities when I am in intense situations in the classroom or consulting room. The standard Western cosmological model of the universe as an impersonal machine does not provide any information or insights at all to help me understand and use these rich experiences.

However, Native American medicine traditions, rooted in the nature mysticism of the Great Mother—who often communicates to her children through dreams—know from millennia of experience that healers and teachers can travel in dreams to other dimensions in their patients' and students' service. For a teacher and counselor, the Native American cosmological model often "buys" a great deal more than a Logos-based cosmology of the Great Father ever could. In both the consulting room and the classroom, the Great Mother speaks to the practitioner who honors her. I have written about various classroom experiences along these lines in my books *Teaching Mysteries* (2004), *Jung and Education* (2005), and *Inside Education* (2007). Here I would like to share another one.

Five years ago I was teaching a cohort of masters students at my university. These students were studying to become principals. This class and I had grown especially close to each other because early in the term I had helped them resolve a serious issue that they had been having. I took on the rather risky role of being their "voice" in a faculty meeting when no one else seemed to be hearing these students' pain about a particular issue—one that had brought the entire class to the brink of quitting the program in exasperation. As their advocate, I was able to broker a solution that satisfied them and got things back on track. Of course, this instantly made me this cohort's favorite teacher.

Because we had grown so close, I decided to share with the class a synchronicity of great moment in my life that I had experienced a decade earlier during my religious conversion. I often tell students about synchronicities that I have had as a teacher, but I almost never share stories of synchronicities that are as personal as this one. Because I had a special bond with this class, however, I took a gamble and told the story.

I began by relating how ten years earlier, during a stormy religious conversion process, I had had a dream about a white dog that walks into my apartment and stands by the television. I then went on to tell them about how I was watching Franco Zeffirelli's movie *The Life of Christ* the day after this dream. While watching it, I picked up a book on the coffee table that I had just borrowed from the personal library of a priest at a nearby parish. As I did so, a card fell out of the book. I picked it up and saw written on it a passage from Jeremiah describing "Rachel lamenting her children" (*NEB*. Jeremiah 31: 15–17). As I read it, a character appeared on the TV screen in front of me and dramatically intoned that very line. (On the other side of the card was a picture of the Virgin Mary.) As if this event were not impressive enough, immediately after the bearded prophetic character on the TV screen had delivered that line, a white dog that I had never seen before in our apartment complex strolled into my ground-level apartment (I had left both the patio gate and my back door open), walked into the living room as if he lived there, and then sat next to the TV, staring over at me quizzically. It was an experience that was both cosmic and comic!

Despite how close this class and I had become, this story was just a little too much for them. Most of them were conservative in terms of religion, tending to look with either disbelief or apprehension on accounts of such paranormal events. In the polite but tense laughter that greeted my account, I could not fail but to register my class' disapproval. My heart sank. I regretted having violated my policy of not relating such personal stories to students. One student, however, who had been rather silent most of the term, rose to the occasion, boldly announcing that she had had many such experiences, too. She thought my story was "very cool!" I appreciated her kind support, but mostly I was just embarrassed by it all and quickly moved the discussion on to the previous night's readings.

The next morning as class began, Paula, my lone advocate from the previous day, asked if she could say something before we began. "Sure, go ahead" I said—secretly apprehensive that she would bring up the white dog story again. And sure enough, she did. "Yesterday as I was driving home from the university, I kept thinking about your dream and about how no one seemed to believe it. It made me feel kind of sad—and a little insecure about my own experiences in the past." "Paula, please stop!" I silently implored her, but what could I do? I had set this thing in motion yesterday with my unwise self-disclosure and was now reaping the consequence of my folly. "You idiot!" I silently chided myself. I had not only discomfited myself, but had caused this woman to doubt her own experiences and now to publicly confess that to the class. What had I done?

But Paula's frown changed to a broad grin as she came to the denouement of her story. "So, there I was, kind of depressed. I pulled up to my house, parked the car in the front yard, and got out. I saw that my husband had not taken the mail out of our box like he usually does. So I went to the box, lifted up the top, and saw that there was a book in it. My reading group had decided on something new to read, but since I haven't been to the group in a long time because I'm so busy with school, I didn't know what the book was. So I took it out of the box, went inside my house, sat down on the couch, and tore off the wrapping. And what do you think I saw?" she asked me and her classmates, searching our puzzled faces. "On the book cover was just one image—a picture of a large white dog!" The class was galvanized. You could have heard the proverbial pin drop.

Just as I had been an advocate for the class previously, now a member was acting as my advocate with the class by showing her colleagues first-hand how synchronicity—which I believe to be a important spiritual phenomenon—worked, especially when, as the Jungian analyst Marvin Spiegelman and the Jungian physicist Victor Mansfeld (1996) have observed, intense emotional ties between people "constellate" archetypal "fields" in such places as consulting rooms and classrooms so that synchronicities happen.

Motivated by the mystery of the Great Mother, I had taken a gamble with my class by sharing a story with them (one that, by the way, involved an archetypal Mother, Rachel, poignantly expressing her love for her children, and Mary, a cosmic Great Mother). This could have easily blown my credibility with my class as a teacher and, even more seriously, made them doubt my commitment to our shared religious faith. That could prove both ecclesiastically and professionally problematic to me at my university, which is the flagship educational site of my faith-community. But the Great Mother, speaking through a female student, saw to it that my gamble was not in vain.

I hope that these personal stories suggest how the intuitive wisdom of the Great Mother is just as important as the intellectual science of the Great Father in our personal and professional circumstances. The Mother's mysticism and artistry must have equal sway in the classroom with the Great Father's theorizing and technology. Theory is necessarily one step removed from nature and the primal encounter to which the Great Mother's intuition and feeling have immediate access.

Of course, synchronicities do not (alas!) happen every day. Still, the Great Mother's empathic, affirming, and therefore healing energy may infuse the classroom on an everyday basis in the care that students feel in what I previously defined as the therapeutic classroom. In such classrooms, the curriculum can promote healing in students because it helps them "surface" and reframe their life-narratives in more positive terms. This can be every bit as miraculous as a synchronicity—and even more so. I will never forget how one middle-aged woman, a recovering alcoholic who had entered teaching in midlife, put it in an interview that I was doing with her for a study. "I see teaching as part of an act of healing—of bringing people to wholeness. When I'm teaching, I am helping to bring each child to wholeness—to their full potential." I can think of no better definition of transformative education than this, nor can I think of a lovelier educational expression of the energy of the Great Mother.

The Great Mother as Artist

Helping a student "re-vision" her life in more heroic terms means helping her restructure her life-narrative. This is an approach to education that uses what Eisner and Vallance (1985) call the self-actualization curricula. Rooted in the humanistic/existentialist psychologies of the 1950s and 1960s, self-actualization curricula stress the importance of "[caring] for the child, that is, [enjoying] him and his growth and self-actualization" (Maslow 1968, 693). As the noted existentialist curricular theorist Maxine Greene (1975) has argued, education must offer the student the "possibility for him as an existing person [to make] sense of his own life-world [by providing] occasions for ordering the materials of that world, for imposing 'configurations' by means of experiences and perspectives made available for personally conducted cognitive action" (299). Such curricula "remind us of what it means for an individual to be present to himself [and] suggest to us the origins of significant quests for meaning" (314). Although Greene believes that any subject-matter can further this pedagogical and therapeutic goal of the narrative-enrichment, she feels the best way to do so is through art. Indeed, to Greene the student's life is a work of art that he, in conjunction with the teacher and his fellow students, is working on in the classroom—like a sculpture being perfected.

A study that I conducted with a colleague in 2002 illustrates Greene's point. We interviewed students in our graduate program who felt that they had been "spiritually called" to become teachers and principals (Mayes and Blackwell Mayes 2002). We wanted to find out what this meant to them, in terms of where they thought it came from and how it impacted their classroom practices. One of the most moving interviews took place with a 36-year-old art teacher—I'll call her "Audrey," a mother of four. She had taught high school for 12 years.

Audrey spoke feelingly about her belief that her calling was twofold: first, to inculcate in her students a love of art ("After all," she said, "God is the ultimate artist and we are his most beautiful works of art!"); and second, to help her students creatively express and deal with the conflicts and conundrums that typify adolescent life by "just try[ing] to let them know I'm there for them to talk to, if they need something, a shoulder to cry on, whatever. . . . 'Just come to me if you have a problem!'"(Mayes and Blackwell Mayes 2002)

As a veteran teacher, Audrey was quite aware of the prohibition against bringing her religious beliefs into the classroom. But as a gifted painter and master teacher, she correctly believed that there was no law against employing the curriculum as a tool of nondogmatic psychospiritual growth in her students—a means of furthering their heroic journeys of discovery of self and others. Audrey saw the curriculum as a way "to get to a more personal level with my kids —their artwork—because sometimes they are using it as therapy to get through a hard time—or to deal with a past experience. They don't even realize why they are doing certain pictures or certain sculptures a certain way."

One form of schooling that relies on the power of artistic symbols to generate hope and foster creativity in students is Waldorf education, developed by Rudolf Steiner. Throughout a Waldorf education, but especially in the earlier years, the teacher organizes much of the curriculum around myths and images from various religions, ranging from relatively unknown indigenous religions to the major world religions. In the early grades, children might group around the teacher and watch her as she paints an image of, say, St. Francis of Assisi while she tells a story of the Saint's life. The students then create an image of St. Francis. During my own visits to Waldorf classrooms, I was struck by how unique each child's representation was. Later, the pictures were hung around the room for all the class to see and collectively comment upon. The pictures were not identified by the names of the individual artists. The teacher explained to me that this was not only to prevent invidious comparison, but also because identifying the artist might inhibit another student from honestly critiquing the artist's piece. For the purpose of the exercise was not only to introduce the children to spiritual symbols and ideas from around the world, but to help each child develop artistically—a process that she felt was inherently spiritual. Even numbers are taught imagistically in the early grades of Waldorf schools by associating them with fairy tales and subtly evoking their archetypal significance in the hearts and minds of the children. Hence, it is felt that the number one appeals to the child's sense of primal unity; two excites the child's unconscious sense of duality; three points mysteriously to conflict, and four to firm grounding (Trostli 1991).[1] By the Waldorf view, then, numbers are an occasion for cultivating "the imaginative basis for an intellectual understanding" (Trostli 1991, 345).

The curricula in the later grades in a Waldorf education continue to rely heavily on symbols. For instance, in the eleventh grade students study the classic medieval romance, *Parzival*, by Wolfram von Eschenbach. Parzival is a noble youth of aristocratic heritage who grows up ignorant of his real station in life. He later discovers and becomes the Lord of the Holy Grail, the chalice that holds the blood of Christ. In so doing, Parzival regains the peace, faith, and dignity that were his original birthright. This story is a metaphor for each of the adolescent students to uniquely mine in their own heroic quest for personal identity and spiritual integration—just as we saw Christy Ann doing with the same legend in her classroom. "In Waldorf schools, the arts are not taught for their own sake; rather they are taught because they allow a child to experience a subject on a level far deeper and richer than the intellectual level" (Trostli 1991, 349).

One is reminded here of the celebrated aesthetician Bendetto Croce's famous statement that the Great Mother's artistic, intuitive ways of knowing form the base upon which the Great Father's analytical knowledge then arises.

> The relation between knowledge or expression and intellectual knowledge or concept, between art and science, poetry and prose, cannot be otherwise defined than by saying that it is one of double degree. The first degree is the expression, the second the concept: the first can stand without the second, but the second cannot stand without the first. There is poetry without prose, but not prose without poetry. Expression, indeed, is the first affirmation of human activity. Poetry is "the mother tongue of the human race"; the first men "were by nature sublime poets." (Vivas and Krieger 1953, 86)

The experience of art invites and incites the student to examine her previous life-narratives and then, using what she has felt and known in the classroom, "compose" an even better one—one that is more fulfilling, generous, and dynamic.

However, a topic, task, or even an entire discipline need not have any obvious connections with art, as such, in order to be handled artistically. Even the sciences (and in many ways *especially* the sciences) are art forms. It is only the banality of materialism that has led us to believe otherwise. Many students are taught the sciences as an empty exercise in memorizing formulas and facts. How different it would be if students were encouraged to see science as an emotionally electric engagement of the whole person with the pulsing, evolving organism of the universe. For, no less than the sculptor or novelist, the scientist in her work channels the archetypal energy of both the Great Mother (in the passion that motivates her inquiries) and the Great Father (in the precision with which she theorizes her findings).

> In one sense, the one who is a scientist is one who lets the object, the phenomenon which is other, love her. She is one who gives up her present ways that she may be formed anew by that strangeness, that otherness before and beyond her. The scientist accepts this incomplete relationship with the world and gives of herself to be drawn out, to be educated or transformed by that which is before her. (Huebner 1999, 367)

The truly creative scientist is not a technician. She is a thinker and a poet, a lover and a channel of both Logos and Eros. In their heroic educational journeys, the teacher and student should cultivate a similar academic ambidexterity, learning to use the right hand of reason and the left hand of intuition.

The Classroom Under the Sign of the Great Mother

The corporate paradigms and programs that increasingly control our educational system are a pedagogical symptom of a larger cultural archetypal imbalance in favor of the Great Father at the expense of the Great Mother (Gellert 2001). Corporate education enshrines competition, technology, and marketability. It consigns to second place the cultivation of compassion, the fostering of respect for others in a democracy, and the developing of intuition and art. It may allow some degree of feeling—but it lavishly rewards dispassionate analysis. It may offer a nod to cultural diversity—but as something that is of only minor importance in the curriculum. Far from nurturing teachers and students as holistic beings, corporate education tends to reduce them to one-dimensional objects to be managed for technocratic purposes. Just as Cremin suggested in 1988, the challenge to education in the twenty-first century would be resisting the metastasis of the military-industrial complex into a military-fiscal-educational one. And just as Joel Spring (1976) warned, U.S. education is increasingly turning into a "sorting machine" spitting out uncritical "worker-citizens" and deciding who should go where in the system.

A pedagogy of the Great Mother offers a way for teachers and students to redress—in the consequential contexts of the classroom—the excessive influence of the Great Father in contemporary American education and culture—and thereby work towards restoring not only a pedagogical balance in the classroom but a political and ethical balance in society at large. I have written in other books about some of the fundamental elements of a pedagogy that honors the Great Mother (Mayes 2003a,b; 2004; 2005; 2007). In this chapter I highlight a few of them, pointing out along the way their indispensability in the student's heroic journey of transformation.

Most importantly, a pedagogy of the Great Mother requires the existence of a therapeutic classroom, where emotion and intuition are honored. Under the sign of the Great Mother, the classroom is a "holding environment," which (as will be recalled from our discussion of Winnicott's theory of child development) is a safe space created by a "good-enough mother." The mother is "good enough" in that she does not expect perfection from either herself or her child. She knows that perfectionism is unrealistic and anxiety-producing. Where everyone must be perfect, no one will dare do anything spontaneous, different, or risky, because the consequences of erring in a perfectionist environment are too dire—ranging from ostracism and shaming to physical punishment.

Perfectionist environments stunt growth and stifle creativity, for growth and creativity are not predictable, neatly packaged affairs. They do not result in a "high score" or "perfect performance" the first time around—if ever. Creative growth does not happen in a clean, straight line from points *A* to *B*, *B* to *C*, and *C* to *D*. It is a natural and organic process—complex, often deep and dark, and steeped in ambiguity. It has to attend to hunches, long-shots. It must flow with the highs and lows, the spurts and slumps, the exhilaration and exhaustion that are part and parcel of making something that is really new.

By definition, anything that comes into being as a risk-free result of uncritically following established procedures cannot be creative. Such a process may produce something that is good and useful, but it does not create anything. Creativity, like any instance of organic maturation, is a messy matter of old growth being sloughed off so that new growth can form. The creative person must cast about, hook onto this intuition or that, let things stew for awhile, and ultimately wind up trying nine approaches that sink before finding that tenth approach that floats. The holding-environments created by good-enough teachers for good-enough students produce the most creative results. In short, education that honors the Great Mother is at home in ambiguity, not distraught at failure, and dedicated above all else to the creation of new life. When the Great Father has unilateral control of a learning environment, then his healthy insistence upon clarity, precision, measurability, and economy becomes excessive, dousing the fire of creativity. In any field, whether it is finite math or the fine arts, the fire of creativity burns best when supplied by both by the oxygen of the Father's in-breathing spirit of theory and the Mother's kindling of intuition and emotion, risk and revolution, art and embodiment.

The Great Mother and Multiculturalism

As a multiculturalist, I believe that multicultural education is one of the most significant manifestations of the reintroduction of the Great Mother into the Western worldview. As with so many of the social issues that became prominent in the 1960s and 1970s—ecology, holistic medicine, natural foods, the anti-war movement, therapy, and women's liberation—multiculturalism evidenced a new collective honoring of the Great Mother's point of view, her organicism, her peace and pace, her respect for all of her children's cultural and spiritual traditions. Thus, in *Understanding the Whole Student: Holistic Multicultural Education* (2007), I and my co-authors have written that multicultural education is more than just about "tolerating" "other" worldviews. It is about the deep honoring and rich sharing of various culture traditions in the forging of a new planetary social order—one that heeds the Great Mother's injunction for all of her children to be respected and loved.

The social theorist Brian Fay (2000) has argued that multiculturalism will prove to be the defining characteristic of the twenty-first century. This is why the advent of the multicultural curriculum is a pivotal event in Western educational theory and practice. It allows nontraditional worldviews that have previously been excluded from the Eurocentric curriculum—relegated to "the null curriculum" (Eisner and Vallance 1985)—to have an equal presence in the classroom. Many of these worldviews—especially those of indigenous, First Nation peoples such as Native Americans—rest upon the Great Mother's penchant for poetry, intuition, and mystery. They share her reverence for nature, treasure her promise of religious ecstasy, and diligently attend to the dreams that she nightly sends as revelations of the inner qualities and ultimate purposes of things.

These Eros-rooted ways of knowing and doing deserve more than just occasional, condescending mention in the Logos-dominated Eurocentric curriculum—although this is what typically happens in what passes for "multicultural education" in American public schooling (Banks and Banks 2001; Nieto 2000). The Eros-affluent worldviews of many First Nation cultures are crucial to any educational process that aims at being archetypally heroic, for to be truly transformative, education must holistically nurture in the student not only the Logos-centered faculty of reason (the intellectual elegance of the theorem), but also the Eros-rooted power of intuition (the transfiguring passion of the poem). As Kant (2007) said in *The Critique of Pure Reason*, human "knowing" is at its best when it is draws upon both "mathetic" rationality and "poetic" sensibility.

Thus, a pedagogy of the Great Mother is inherently multicultural. It creates the classroom conditions in which students can see themselves and others from multiple perspectives. This matures students emotionally, hones them intuitively, and frees them from outdated, overly restrictive, or simply parochial cultural practices that keep them from thinking outside the socioeconomic box into which they were born. The importance of such an ability in our increasingly interconnected world can hardly be overstated.

The multicultural pedagogies of the Great Mother evidence her maternal wisdom in encouraging her children to see the universe, and their place in it, with ever newer eyes. Like any good mother, the Great Mother (as the feminine face of God) loves all of her children and insists that, as siblings, they find ways to play, create, and grow together. The Great Mother gives birth to classrooms where, because diverse cultural points of view are cherished and explored, students learn to resist the totalitarian tendency that is inherent in any culturally absolutist worldview—namely, to see the "Fatherland" as supreme and other cultures as more or less inferior—in need of "saving" (which usually means "colonizing"). In the Great Mother's pedagogy virtually any subject or issue in the curriculum, from marketing to metaphysics, represents an occasion for students to articulate various cultural views on that topic so that each student may uniquely weave them all together into an existentially transformative and personally meaningful vision.

An archetypally balanced, multicultural pedagogy includes the following assumptions:

- Holistic multicultural education is important for all students and teachers—especially in the postmodern world of the twenty-first century.
- There are culturally variable yet equally valid ways of viewing what it means to teach and learn; this means that there are multiple ways of reasoning and therefore multiple means of teaching and assessing students in order to accommodate cultural variability.
- It is important for teachers to honor and cultivate valid cultural differences in their students (even though a single teacher cannot, of course, be expected to know precisely what all those differences are) and to be willing to explore those differences and encourage students to do the same thing.
- If teachers are not aware of these differences and do not approach them holistically and sensitively, they can misinterpret and mislabel student behavior (categorizing a student as "cognitively deficient," for instance, when in fact she is merely "cognitively different"); this can lead to the disastrous educational practice of treating students from non-dominant cultures in a way that alienates them and incites behavior and attitudes that are damaging to both the student, the teacher, and the school culture.

- If teachers strive with students to become as aware as possible of the valid cultural differences that exist, and honor and celebrate alternative ways of knowing and learning (all the while avoiding an unnecessary and destructive moral relativism), then they will help create an enriching classroom environment that is more physically, emotionally, ethically, and spiritually nurturing for all students.
- Along with their students, teachers must examine their own cultural assumptions, beliefs, and biases by engaging in what the educational anthropologists George and Louise Spindler (1992) have called *cultural reflectivity*; this involves joining with their students in becoming "ethnographic investigators" (Heath 1983) of each other's cultures.
- It is important to teach the dominant culture's norms and official bodies of "knowledge" in order to politically and professionally empower all students; however, it is equally important—for members and non-members of the dominant cultural group—to critique those norms. (Adapted from Mayes et al. 2007, 7–8)

THE GREAT FATHER

One way of identifying the characteristics of the Great Father comes from Jungian typology. The reader will recall that Jungian personality theory posits four basic types—thinking, feeling, sensate, and intuitive—and two basic attitudes—introversion and extroversion. In examining the pedagogy of the Great Mother, the emphasis has been on introverted feeling and intuition—the poetic predisposition.

On the other hand, the archetypally male principle is an extraverted attitude employing thinking and sensation (that is, rationality and empiricism). It looks outward towards people and things as phenomena to be analyzed, systematized, and operated upon. It prizes conceptual elegance and parsimony above all else, and it aims at shaping the world of physical and social "entities" according to sound theoretical principles that yield measurable empirical results. At once sublimely abstract and relentlessly pragmatic, the archetypal male principle is syllogistic and results-oriented. In academic terms, the male principle is generally thought to shine forth most clearly in fields such as philosophy, mathematics, physics, biology, economics, and law (in both their theoretical and applied forms).

Elements of a Pedagogy of the Great Father

The archetypally male principle of Logos manifests itself educationally in curricula that have been characterized as "academic-rationalist" (Eisner and Vallance 1985), "intellectual-academic" (Ornstein and Hunkins 1988), and "interpretive-procedural" (Mayes 2003a). I have suggested some dangers of relying exclusively upon Logos as the sole criterion of a good curriculum. In doing so, I have drawn attention to the "shadow side" of the archetype of the Great Father: The Senex (Jung 1963)—beautifully captured in Dickens's character of Scrooge. The Senex is a joyless old man—pinched, dry, rule-bound, greedy, and spiritless. These are symptoms of the degradation of the luminescent Logos of the Great Father into to the legalism and literalism of the Senex—his potential for mischief when he wields unilateral power.

However, a balanced pedagogy also equally honors the Great Father. It insists upon the crucial educational importance of "the formal conversation" of rational academic discourse (Noddings 1999), the transformative dialogical approach to "the curriculum as transaction" (Miller 1988). The pedagogical Great Father must be equally present in the classroom as the Great Mother if there is to be that marriage of archetypal energies that is essential to transformative education—and, indeed, to individuation in all of its forms. There is power in the portrayal of the student as a philosopher—as seen in such important works as Lipman's (1988) *Philosophy Goes to School* and Adler's (1982) *The Paideia Proposal.* My focus on education under the sign of Eros has simply been designed to put Logos into context—and into balance with Eros (which is decidedly not the case today).

It is essential to transformative education that the student encounter and learn to love the Great Father in the Father's pure aspect, for it is the Great Father who establishes the conventions and provides the potentials of formal academic discourse. Only then will the student be able to use (as well as critique) the standards texts, theories, worldviews, and applications of the "canonical curriculum" in her existential growth. Certainly, as an instrument of colonization, the traditional curriculum is a great danger as I have argued above. But as part of the student's complete educational equipment on the road of heroic existential challenge and change, Logos-based knowledge is every bit as important to her as Eros-based knowledge.

A danger in certain of the more radical multicultural approaches to education is that they seem to want to dismiss Logos education as merely a tool of white academic colonialism (Crenshaw 1995). I agree that, in excess, a Logos curriculum does lead to that problem. However, Logos is primarily a cosmic fact, not a political one. Logos is also a core psychospiritual fact—one of the two major poles in the creative Logos-Eros interaction that produces thoughts and feelings and generates "psychic energy" (Harding 1973). A pedagogy that minimizes Logos is as philosophically indefensible and archetypally imbalanced as one that minimizes Eros. Furthermore, to dismiss (in a polemically anti-Logos swing) traditional Western education as irrelevant and oppressive is politically naive. As W. E. B. Dubois said long ago, in somewhat different terms but to the same effect, a Logos-weak education impoverishes precisely those students who most need it to advance socioeconomically through access to prestigious knowledge and skills.

We saw elements of the pedagogy of the Great Father in our previous discussion of teachers as master cognitive-artisans. As Wise Elders, they guide their young cognitive apprentices down the heroic road of learning, showing them how to think like experts in a given field do (Bruner 1960; Resnick 1987). In this way, students internalize the cognitive structures and procedural conventions of a discipline—its "mode of representation, economy, and power" (Bruner 1960, 44). No less an educational luminary than John Dewey—who is often unjustly accused of not valuing cognitive rigor in the curriculum—insisted that students must learn how to think logically by: "1. becoming aware of a difficulty (or a felt difficulty), 2. identifying the problem, 3. assembling and classifying data and formulating hypotheses, 4. accepting or rejecting the tentative hypotheses, and 5. formulating conclusions and evaluating them" (cited in Ornstein and Hunkins 1988, 79).

When students under the teacher's guidance engage in processes such as these, then classrooms become communities of rational discourse—Deweyan laboratories of democracy where students learn how to create knowledge that will move them forward into ever widening realms of intellectual and social possibility. "Even young children can enter into such dialogue," writes Lipman, for "doing philosophy is not a matter of age, but of ability to reflect scrupulously and courageously on what one finds important." Teaching students to think philosophically should thus be "the core or armature of the curriculum" (Lipman 1988, 249). Of the thirty critical skills that Lipman wants student to acquire, he particularly stresses: "(1) concepts; (2) generalizations; (3) cause-effect relationships; (4) inferences; (5) consistencies and contradictions; (6) analogies; (7) part-whole and whole-part connections; (8) problem formulations; (9) reversibility of logical statements; and (10) application of principles to real-life situations" (cited in Ornstein and Hunkins 1988, 98).

Although Lipman's vision of curriculum entails serious devotion to logic, his idea of the "reasonable curriculum" is far from boring. Thinking reasonably also means thinking creatively, picturing new worlds and then creating them. This is something that students, still flush with youthful optimism, not only can do, but very much want to do, as long as they are allowed to consider issues that are personally and socially relevant:

> There is good reason to think that the model of each and every classroom—that which it seeks to approximate and at times becomes—is the community of inquiry. By inquiry, of course, I mean perseverance in self-corrective exploration of issues that are felt to be both important and problematic. . . . If we begin with the practice in the classroom—the practice of converting it into a reflective community that thinks in the disciplines about the world and about its thinking about the world, we soon come to recognize that communities can be nested within larger communities and these within larger communities still, if all hold the same allegiance to the same procedure of inquiry. There is the familiar ripple effect outward, like the stone thrown in the pond: wider and wider, more and more encompassing communities are formed, each community consisting of individuals committed to self-corrective exploration and creativity. (Lipman 1988, 252)

Another manifestation of the Great Father in a balanced pedagogy includes approaches that aim at getting students to examine their own cognitive "maps" about some topic or subject so that they can compare those maps to the ones that the "experts" in a field have in their minds. In so doing, students can alter their cognitive maps according to the gold standard of the expert's map. In cognitive psychology, cognitive maps are called "schemas." Rummelhart, a leading schema theorist, defines a schema theory as:

> a theory about how knowledge is represented and about how that representation facilitates the use of knowledge in particular ways. According to schema theories, all knowledge is packaged into units. These units are the schemata. Embedded in these packets of knowledge is, in addition to the knowledge itself, information about how this knowledge is to be used. A schema, then, is a data structure for

> representing the generic concepts stored in memory. There are schemata representing our knowledge about all concepts: those underlying objects, situations, events, sequences of events, actions, and sequences of actions. A schema contains, as part of its specification, the network of interrelations that is believed to normally hold among the constituents of the concept in question. (1980, 141)

All of these powerful pedagogical theories and practices and more are included in the student's necessary encounter with the universal brilliance of the Great Father.

BRINGING THE GREAT FATHER INTO BALANCE WITH THE GREAT MOTHER

As the archetypally male principle of the sun, Logos's splendid mission is to cast the light of logic into the dark nooks and crannies of the universe. However, when Eros is disprized, then individuals and societies are prone to dismiss as meaningless, even dangerous, any mystery that does not yield its enshrouded feminine secrets to logic's penetrating masculine rays. When the Great Father's solar power is not in balance with the subtler lunar influence of the Great Mother—represented by the magnetic pull of the moon and the fertile darkness of the unconscious—then the result can only be a flood of masculine light so intense that it ultimately blinds and burns rather than illuminates.

Just as the universe must give up some of its secrets to the light of reason, so must the light of reason know its limitations and revere the enriching spiritual enchantments of the fertile darkness. There must be a rhythm of day and night—in the soul as well as in nature in general. Achieving a dynamic equipoise of the maternal moon of intuition and emotion with the paternal sun of geometrical analysis and functionality was what Jung meant by "individuation." It is the precondition of health and growth—and is also the heart of heroic education.

Nevertheless, Western education tends to privilege reason over all other ways of processing and acting on one's world. In many ways this is especially true of U.S. culture (Gellert 2001). This is an unhealthy state of affairs because it promotes over-intellectualization, rewarding the student for living entirely "upstairs" in his brain, alienated from the other aspects of his total being. As I have argued in my book *Seven Curricular Landscapes: An Approach to the Holistic Curriculum*:

> Instead of being allowed to resolve basic physical and emotional issues at a natural pace, children are increasingly forced to acquire information and cognitive skills at a breakneck speed that runs roughshod over healthy developmental rhythms. Instead of engaging in those relational activities that are the most fertile ground for the blossoming of the child's early physical, emotional, imaginative, and verbal potentials, he must devote growing numbers of hours, even in the earliest grades, to memorization and acquiring skills that will allow him to "test well." This collective national fixation upon high scores on norm-referenced tests is particularly damaging when it comes to the very young, resulting in what some public health officials are calling "the new morbidity" among children. The excessive use of Ritalin and similar drugs in our schools today—those chemicals that constitute a pharmaceutical extra-curriculum of control—is a consequence of our political economy. (Mayes 2003, 40–41)

Fairbairn's statement that over-intellectualization is pathological reflects "a general tendency on the part of individuals with a schizoid component to heap up their values in an inner world" (1992, 8). When this happens—when, that is, cognition supplants (instead of balances) emotion and intuition—then the intellect changes from a powerful tool of creation into a weapon of domination. It comes to represent a way of hiding in a bloodless, passionless world of theory in order to avoid the task of developing deep self-awareness and rich relationship with others. In its extreme forms, this overvaluation of thought can even be characterized as schizoid (Fairbairn 1992, 20).

The cure for this individual and cultural malady is to begin to more deeply honor the lunar rhythms of the Great Mother—her nocturnal periodicities of receptivity, reflectivity, rest, and regeneration—for these are the cosmic forces that inform feminine biology and power the archetypally feminine psyche. We must celebrate the Great Mother as a co-equal partner with the Great Father in constituting one Godhead, resisting the West's cultural tendency to consign the archetypally feminine principle to the outer reaches of psyche and society. As Jung never tired of arguing, the male must honor his anima in order to achieve balance—a fact that is no less true of a society than of the individuals who comprise it. Although Jung was the first modern psychologist to theorize this fact and put it into clinical practice, he was by no means the first person to recognize this ominous imbalance in Western culture.

Mary Shelley's famous novel about Dr. Frankenstein and his bizarre creation was a cautionary tale for Western culture in the first half of the nineteenth century with its rapidly growing industrialism (Abrams 1973). Dr. Frankenstein symbolizes the Western tendency to live so excessively in the world of abstraction and technology that it threatens to misshape people and the world. This is what happens in Dr. Frankenstein's ultimate experiment. He attempts to use the archetypally masculine power of science to supplant the sacred feminine power of creating life. This mocking of the feminine principle results in an unnatural birth—that of the monster Frankenstein, who is a grotesque exaggeration of the male principle. As the Age of Science and Technology was gaining momentum at the beginning of the nineteenth century, Mary Shelley was warning about the terrible possibilities that could arise as a result of the imbalance of the masculine and feminine, of Logos and Eros.

I believe that the cosmos in its wisdom often provides humanity with archetypal lessons that it hides in world events and leaves us to uncover and decipher. The explosion of the space shuttle Challenger on January 28 1986, in addition to being a tragedy in its own right, offered us just such lesson about the perils of archetypal imbalance. And as fate would have it, it involved a teacher.

As the first member of the Teacher in Space Program, Christa MacAuliffe was the media focus of this historic launching. She was at the center of the world's gaze that lovely January day at 11:37 a.m.—an hour when the sun, the classical symbol of Logos, had almost reached its zenith. However, the world's fascinated delight at this marvel of Western ingenuity turned to shock as a female teacher, a fitting symbol of the feminine principle, was blown to bits (along with the rest of the shuttle's crew, of course) while her young students, huddled around a television in the classroom where she had taught them, looked on in disbelief and then horror.

The penetrating male thrust of the launch was scientifically designed to hurl Christa into space atop a titanic solid-rocket booster—both an actual product and a phallic symbol of Western science, technology, and its (literally) "ex-orbitant" wealth. Here, in the form of this missile, was a proud, even arrogant image of Logos defiant, coopting the female principle, encasing her in the synthetic environment of an artificial capsule. As its very name implied, the shuttle's archetypal mission was to "challenge" the eternal, nocturnal mysteries of the universe—to see if it was possible to make the Great Mother yield her secrets to the genius of Western science and technology—to forcibly penetrate her. The result, in Christa's death, was the destruction of the female principle of nurturance and care and the psycho-spiritual maiming of her children-students.

As I watched the videos of this disaster over and over, I saw the shuttle and booster explode into pieces, then drift down in slow, defeated spirals (but with a kind of eerie grace) into the eternal, amniotic waters of the Great Mother-Ocean, calmly waiting to receive her over-reaching children back into herself. Each time I did so, the message came through with painful clarity: when the Great Father is not in close, loving, and reverent contact with his Eternal Mate —the Great Mother—the consequences, however dazzling in the short-run, must be apocalyptic in the final resort.

The Union of Rex and Regina

The union of Logos and Eros engenders heroic education. This is why, Jung noted, Renaissance alchemical texts often pictured the culmination of alchemy's intellectual-spiritual work (the production of the "Philosopher's Stone" or "Spiritual Gold") in a painting or engraving of an archetypal King and Queen—Rex and Regina—intertwined in the act of making love. In heroic education, it is the student who is the Philosopher's Stone and Spiritual Gold—the unique offspring of the eternal joining of Eros and Logos, Yin and Yang, Moon and Sun, Great Mother and Father.

Jung's early research in archetypal gender psychology paved the way for later psychologists to explore, in their own terms, the significance of the Great Mother in psychic functioning. Carol Gilligan (1982), for instance, has proposed that women tend to see morally complex situations more in terms of how supportively people "care for" each other than how exactly they follow an external code of "law." Other feminist psychologists have emphasized what the feminist psychologist Mary Belenkey has called "women's ways of knowing" (Belenkey et al. 1986), which she sees as being relational and intuitive. Of course, it would be simplistic to claim that every woman's psyche operates totally under the influence of the Great Mother and every man's totally under that of the Great Father. Gilligan's and Belenkey's message is simply that: (1) women's psychodynamics tend toward the pole of the Great Mother and men's toward the Great Father, and (2) everyone's psyche is to some degree a mix of archetypally female and male elements.

Jung was the first twentieth century psychologist to make these ideas a core feature of clinical theory and practice—as the reader will recall from Chapter 2, in which we looked at Jung's insistence on the need for a male to integrate his inner-feminine, or anima, to achieve psychospiritual completeness and liberation, as well as the need for a female to integrate her inner-masculine, or animus, to become whole. Since the 1960s, this principle of Jungian psychology has begun to make its presence felt in popular culture. Many men and women have become much more conscious of contrasexual elements within themselves that had previously been repressed due to strict gender-role definitions.

In a 1938 article, "Psychological Aspects of the Mother Complex," Jung talked (in terms which were culturally and politically bold for the times) about why it is necessary for a man to honor and incorporate the archetypal energy of Eros in his psyche. Interestingly, Jung related this to being a teacher:

> It gives him a great capacity for friendship, which often creates ties of astonishing tenderness between men and may even rescue friendship between the sexes from the limbo of the impossible. He may have good taste and an aesthetic sense which are fostered by the presence of a feminine streak. Then he may be supremely gifted as a teacher because of his almost feminine insight and tact. . . . Often he is endowed with a wealth of religious feelings . . . and a spiritual receptivity which makes him responsive to revelation. (see Jung 1968a, 86–87)

Similarly, the woman who discovers and cultivates her inner masculine energy is more likely to know her own mind, be healthily assertive, set clear goals that she efficiently attains, and refuse to allow herself to be physically or emotionally demeaned by a manipulative man. A woman who has integrated her animus is in touch with her power and knows how to use it well.

One of Jung's greatest contributions to twentieth century thought was his insistence that both individually and socially we must find ways to maintain a balance between the male and female principles, each principle finding its completion in its interaction with and support of the other. How can the teacher accomplish this in his classroom practice?

An Archetypally Balanced Pedagogy

Heroic pedagogy requires that students encounter and learn to honor both the Great Mother and the Great Father in their academic adventure. The instructional theorist Jere Brophy (1994) offers a superb approach to achieving this balance in teaching and learning. He demonstrates that best educational practices are, like the best parenting styles, authoritative (see also Conger and Galambos 1997).

We can understand what an authoritative parenting or teaching style is by looking at the concepts of "demand" and "care." It is the Great Father who demands excellent and usable work from his children. It is the Great Mother who carefully provides love and nurturance. Where the Great Father is unilaterally in charge, there is, as Brophy puts it, high demand but low care. This is an authoritarian form of governance. It prepares students to live under a despot. It is anti-democratic and anti-heroic, because it does not allow the individual to develop in health and freedom. The opposite error is to govern in a way that has high care but only low demands, if any. This permissive form of governance, which is the result of the Great Mother being exclusively in charge, is also inconsistent with personal individuation or political democracy. It breeds irresponsibility and provides neither a stimulus for growth in the individual nor the structure to contain that growth so that it does not become chaotic.

However, when the Great Father and the Great Mother, acting together as equal archetypal partners, have the same say and sway in a classroom, then students experience the miracle of authoritative teaching. Authoritative teachers expect great things from their students. They insist that their students attain their "personal bests" regarding a certain task, topic, or field (understanding that any given student's personal best will vary from field to field depending upon her interest and ability in it). In other words, such teachers are "high demand."

But they are also "high care." Authoritative teachers relate lovingly and authentically with their students. They are in touch with their own emotions and intuitions, and thus know how to help students access and cultivate theirs as well. They are not afraid to assess a student's work, but they insist upon assessment that is authentic, varied, rich, non-punitive, and supportive of the student's ongoing development as a complete existential being. This means that they will not assess their students in ways that they deem to be harmful to them—which, of course, is precisely the malignant effect that corporate forms of standardized education have on the student.

The classrooms of authoritative teachers are "holding environments"—cognitively challenging yet emotionally safe spaces where students not only succeed, but can also be allowed to encounter difficulties—and occasionally even to "fail"—so that they can firmly but lovingly be shown how to regroup and grow. Such teachers know that it is not necessary to be perfect. Indeed, they know that perfectionism is toxic. They simply do their best—in not only their teaching, but in their own research—to be intellectually rigorous as well as emotionally generous, striving to discover how to balance those two goals. Such teachers are generally successful and satisfied in their jobs, because they are working in a manner that unites their and their students' hearts and minds in a shared, heroic adventure of discovery in the classroom.

On the road of academic adventure, students, shaped by their encounters with both the Great Mother and Father in the archetypally balanced classroom, have intensive and extensive opportunities throughout their classroom adventure to see and internalize both the maternal and paternal principles—the poetic and mathetic, the intuitive and analytical, Eros and Logos. This encounter with the Great Mother and Father brings them to the climax of their trek—the Supreme Reward. To understand what this reward is, we turn now to Jung's idea of "the transcendent function."

THE TRANSCENDENT FUNCTION: THE SUPREME TASK AND GREAT PRIZE

Jeffrey Miller (2004) has correctly claimed that the idea of the transcendent function is the most pivotal one in all of Jung's writing—the very heart of his work. Being able to use the transcendent function in one's life is the culmination of Jungian therapy. It is also the culmination of the heroic educational journey. What is the transcendent function?

It should be made clear that Jung's use of the word "transcendent" does not necessarily mean "otherworldly"—although the operation of the transcendent function may lead to a more spiritual point of view. Rather, Jung simply means that where there are two opposing elements involved in resolving an intellectual, emotional, or moral tension, the truth is to be found in a third position that unites those opposites in a higher synthesis. This higher synthesis is the transcendent function. For Jung, these two fundamentally (indeed, eternally) "opposing elements" are: (1) the extraverted thinking-sensing complex that constitutes the archetypally masculine principle and (2) the introverted feeling-intuition complex that constitutes the archetypally feminine principle. What is more, according to Jung the male functions of thinking and sensing are conscious processes while feeling and intuition grow out of the unconscious. The transcendent function therefore also represents the healthy interaction of conscious and unconscious factors in the psyche—another definition of integration and individuation. In other words, the transcendent function is fundamentally an archetypal integration of the Great Father and Mother, Logos and Eros, mind and heart.

As the reader will recall, Jung's idea of "individuation"—psycho-spiritual completeness and health—is that it combines contrary elements within the psyche into an organic whole. This is the way that Jung psychologically interpreted Jesus's injunction: "Be ye perfect" (*NEB*. Matthew 5: 48). As Jung pointed out, the Greek word τελειωσ [teleios], which Matthew has Jesus use in this passage, does not really mean "perfect" so much as it means "perfected" in the sense of having arrived at a goal, having accomplished a purpose, and having matured to completion. What Jesus was really saying, Jung wisely concluded, was not that Jesus was insisting that a human being must be sinless, (an impossible goal in this life, and another example of the Great Father in his unforgiving aspect as the Senex), but must be individuated—must complete her heroic cycle in becoming a wiser, kinder, stronger, and more efficacious person, one who has learned, and will continue to learn, those crucial lessons that make her sagacious in this life and prepare her for even greater stature and scope in the life beyond. For:

> truly compassionate and creative attitudes and behaviors (still the best working definition of virtue) grow not out of being perfect (which is, in any case, impossible) but from being whole, which was . . . Jung's . . . preferred translation of τελειωσ [teleios]. Not by being perfect, said Jung, but by being whole—facing and integrating the imagery and energy of the individual and collective unconscious [with the rational processes of the conscious mind]—could a person become mature, compassionate, and potent. (Mayes and Blackwell Mayes 2005, 88)

Of course, all of this is also at the very heart of the processes and purposes of transformative education. Being "synonymous with progressive development towards a new attitude" (Jung 1953, 99), the transcendent function is the goal of transformative education. It is the hero's "Supreme Task." This heroic task—educational in the broadest sense because it involves one's entire life—is never fully accomplished in one class, nor in a lifetime of classes, nor in any other specific moment in life itself, for the education this life provides us is not over until one's last breath is drawn. But one's commitment to the process can be, and indeed must be, total and uncompromising if one is to lead an existentially authentic life—a life that fully engages the often exasperating, but always fertile, complexities that make up our mysterious existence on this planet.

This moral commitment to truly engage with life in good faith through the intelligent and compassionate use of the Transcendent Function is the "Great Gift" that the hero wins. It is the "Heroic Sword," the "Pearl of Great Prince," the "Crown," "Magical Amulet," and "Ultimate Boon." It is the hero's reward, won on his existential pilgrimage towards greater truth and knowledge. It is this that empowers him to constantly renew himself and the world, and thereby (as the Buddha counseled in his final sermon) work out his own salvation, and aid in that of others, as we individually and collective pass over the rough trails of this existence into a time beyond time and a place beyond place.

Archetypal Reflectivity in the Service of the Transcendent Function: A Personal Example

I hope the reader will not mind that I give an example of the Transcendent Function from my own life as a teacher. It is a series of dreams I had at a time when I was attempting to work out a balance between the Great Mother and Great Father not only in my classroom life, but in general.

Several years ago, I was writing a book, one which my students now say that they like because they feel that it blends theory and practice: it is neither so abstract that it does not apply to their actual situations as teachers and principals, nor so "practical" as to be just another overly technical "how to" manual. What they do not know is that this book would have been very imbalanced on the side of theory if I not had the following series of three dreams while writing it.

In the first dream, I am lecturing to a class on Aristotle. But something is wrong. I can feel it. I look to my left and see an old high school friend of my youth, Arnold Palacios, a Chicano with whom I had been involved in both political and artistic activities throughout my teenage years. He is looking on with a mixture of disappointment and irony while I am making this very dry presentation on the Greeks to my class. I ask him to leave and he does.

In the dream, Arnold Palacios represented the emotional, political, and artistic richness of my life as a young man. To emphasize this point in the dream, he is standing on the left side of me. The left is classically associated with the feminine principle and the right with the masculine. The message in this image was that I was banishing my connection with the feminine functions of emotion, multicultural richness, and artistic creativity through my overly analytical, ultimately sterile, and therefore existentially unproductive obsession with "theory." Arnold is a person whom I have always admired because of his ability as a man to elegantly and potently access the feminine principle in order to be an integrated and effective thinker and activist. I was obviously at a point in life where, if I did not honor all of the parts of my existence, they would strike back with a vengeance.

My next dream in this series occurred a few nights later. I am on the beach, the waves beautifully lapping at my feet. I am walking with Arnold, but get separated from him somehow. My son, Joshua, is with him, but I know that Joshua will be fine, so I am not at all worried about that. Trying to contact them, however, I simply cannot figure out how to operate my cell phone. It keeps showing me all sorts of mathematical symbols and numbers, but it will not allow me to find Arnold's number and call him to contact him and my son. Exasperated, I begin to notice that there is a swelling on my right arm—first as a small bump, then as a large one, and finally covering my whole forearm.

I walk into a pharmacy. Everything is white, antiseptic, with bottles of gray pills neatly shelved on aluminum racks. I realize that the swelling is the symptom of a heart attack. The pharmacist, not very interested in what is going on with me, calls one of his female colleagues. I am hopeful that she will do something to aid me, but she becomes involved with another customer in some sort of large business deal and forgets about me. I then wake up.

This dream was confirming the message of the previous one: If I get separated from "the balanced male" (Arnold) with whom I must develop strong ties of communication and love (symbolized by my son) in order to access the archetypally female principle (the ocean), then there will be hell to pay. And that is just what happens in the dream. I am unable to contact Arnold and my son because I can only see abstract mathematical symbols. I have lost touch with my heart. It therefore "attacks" me in order to catch my attention.[2]

My solution in the dream to the problem is all wrong. Indeed, the solution is a symptom of the problem itself. I walk into a pharmacy—a symbol to me of allopathic Western medicine, which, although undoubtedly a marvel, can become a monster if it does not take into account all aspects of the patient's life, not just the physical symptoms and the magical chemical bullets to eradicate them. In other words, my dream was warning me against the temptation to fall into total Logos with its inordinate focus on the creation of systems and products (the gray pills neatly stacked on stainless steel).

The dream does provide a hint of the solution to this problem in the form of the female pharmacist (the introduction of the feminine principle as a balance to the male principle). But the female principle has itself been co-opted in my dream (and therefore in myself) by the Logos approach (she is dressed in a lab coat) and its tempting offer of financial success, symbolized by her business deal. This last fact probably symbolized the fact that I was at that point being more motivated by the prospect of professional rewards in writing the book than by how I could aid my own heroic existential growth and hopefully that of my readers.

The next night, I had the final dream in this trio of messages from my subconscious and unconscious. Now Arnold is the one who is teaching Aristotle. I am sitting with my students, enjoying his lecture. While listening, I look around the class and see that the students are enthralled with his vibrant and humorous presentation of Aristotle, which, although it handles the Greek philosopher's ideas brilliantly, also includes large measures of passion, humor, and contemporary political applications. He alternates between Spanish (a language that I speak and love) and English in his lecture. In Spanish, he mentions a passage from the book he is lecturing on. I pick up my copy of the book from my desk to refer to that passage and see that the book is simply entitled *Aristotle*, written on a light pink cover. I wake up feeling good.

This dream offers the solution to my dilemma. I can study and engage theoretical issues in my research, writing, and teaching. However, I must always do so with large doses of humor in order not to take myself too seriously, as well as to make the material interesting to my students. My scholarship and teaching must also be true to my heart. Spanish is the most "heartful" language I have ever known and one that I grew up hearing throughout my youth as a child of the American Southwest, living next to the Barrios of South Tucson. I grew up immersed in the beauty of Mexican American culture—its focus on family, passion, music, and painting; its veneration of saints and unwavering loyalty to friends; and above all, its maternal mysticism in its devotion to Mary, Mother of God. In other words, the dream is grounding my tendency towards rational analysis (Aristotle) in the feminine principle (the pink background). With Logos thus grounded in Eros, I can (so my dream is telling me) come closer to my ideal of teaching, writing, and living in ways that promote intuitive, emotional, and spiritual development in myself and others.

While researching and writing this chapter, I had another dream which warned me that, although it is true that the Great Mother has been marginalized and that it is necessary to reinstate her as an equal force, I must also resist the counter-tendency to overcompensate for this injustice by holding her up so high that I begin to marginalize the Great Father—a lifelong temptation for me. This dream emphasized the need for archetypal balance. It stressed that marginalizing the Great Father in the classroom is just as destructive of the heroic educational process as is marginalizing the Great Mother.

In this final dream, I am sitting in the house where I grew up as a young boy. I am in the kitchen. Apparently, my mother had made a delicious meal. I ate too much of it and now feel uncomfortable, even a little sick. I then notice that one of my former dissertation students, a Hawaiian woman, is sitting in front of me. She begins to insist that I do much more than is really appropriate for me as her advisor in order to get her dissertation in shape. In effect, she wants me to "co-author" her dissertation, because she does not feel able to do the whole thing by herself. I tell her "no." In Hawaiian, she says something very nasty to me. I order her to leave my house. She does. I then notice that I have a textbook on cognitive psychology. I look forward to reading it.

In this dream, I am in danger of "taking in" and "putting out" too much of the maternal principle. I have overeaten the fare provided by the mother. In consuming too much of the maternal principle, I become ill. The ancient Greek physicians believed that disease was caused by an imbalance of the basic elements in the body. Today we understand this idea to be symbolic of the need for a balance of archetypal elements in the psyche in order to achieve emotional health. My nausea in the dream results from an imbalance in favor of the feminine. And just as I have taken in too much of the maternal principle in the dream, now a Hawaiian woman is demanding excessive mothering from me. The "maternal-complex" core of this dream is emphasized by the fact that the woman is Hawaiian, because I think of Polynesian cultures as generally quite matriarchal. This matriarch wants me to actually write her dissertation for her! This would go beyond healthily supporting her as a student. It would be coddling her and thereby preventing her own heroic growth. I would be falling into the dysfunctional role of an academic "enabler," not rising to my calling as a mentor. I would also be violating the law of the Great Father—my obligation to the scholarly community of which I am a part to be honest in my work and to make sure that my students are honest in theirs.

Drawing excessively upon the female principle, and giving excessively to a student because one is possessed and inflated by that principle, represents the shadow side of the Great Mother archetype. This is the infamous Devouring Great Mother. She controls her children by inducing guilt and dependence through her excessive nurturance of them (Neumann 1954). Under the guise of love, she consumes her children to satisfy her own need for validation and control. In real life, children of devouring mothers often never really cut themselves psychologically loose from their mothers.

I have found in counseling young couples that this is a common problem. The young man cannot fully psychologically commit to his wife because he is fundamentally still "married" to his mother psychically. Or, the young woman cannot really begin an authentic partnership with her husband because she still values her mother's opinions about how they as a young couple should lead their lives more than she does the conclusions that she and her husband had previously reached—conclusions over which the Devouring Mother seems to have veto power.

In the dream, I banish this excess from my psychic "house" and begin to read a textbook in cognitive psychology. Cognitive psychology deals with how concepts are formed and how invalid concepts can be changed through an essentially rational process. Cognitive psychology is in the domain of the Great Father. In the dream, the Great Father (in the form of a textbook symbolizing my life as a teacher and my need to honor the archetypally masculine principle in my own "psychology") injects a healthy dose of unsentimental clarity into a situation that might otherwise degenerate into sentimentality and irrational guilt—the dark flip side of the archetypally feminine principle.

In education, as in everything, balance is key; and key to transformative education is the equipoise of Eros and Logos in the classroom, empowering the student to evolve intellectually and emotionally, pragmatically and ethically, professionally and spiritually. Education that honors both heart and mind, poetry and science, the Great Mother and the Great Father, fosters the creative dialectical tension and archetypal balance that define individuation—and heroic education.

NOTES

1. See also von Franz (1974) for more on the archetypes of numbers.

2. I have found in counseling others that such dreams are often actual warnings of an impending physical problem and must therefore be taken seriously through a change in the client's lifestyle. This is a point that Jung often made.

CHAPTER 6

Conclusion

The archetypal educational cycle

Despite the fact that every classroom is unique, an educational world unto itself, it is still theoretically and pragmatically useful to talk about some general patterns that exist in "the process of education" (Bruner 1960). These patterns vary, depending upon how the goals of education are being defined. If what is wanted is students who can score well on standardized tests or perform a certain mechanical task efficiently, then the pattern of stimulus-response and the rhythms of reinforcement schedules are relevant. However, if what is sought is the growth of the whole student in existential authenticity, emotional richness, and critical acuity, then there is, I believe, no better way to frame teaching and learning than as an archetypal hero's journey—the ancient narrative framework that elegantly renders the stages and tasks of deep transformation.

In this study, we have tracked the journey of the teacher and student in their joint odyssey of holistic evolution. The trek begins with the novitiate hearing a call. If the call is genuine—one that promises existential deepening—then, as the clear clarion sound of high adventure, it rings true and the student generally resonates to it. For those students who resist the summons, however, there are often psychosocial factors at play. To overcome these requires that the teacher come to the classroom situation armed with psychodynamic and cultural knowledge—and be able to use it sensitively in establishing a therapeutic classroom. If, however, the call is false—if it is merely a preface to a program of control, a pedagogy objectifying teachers and students—then resisting that call is emotionally, politically, intellectually, and morally imperative.

Yet even when the call is true—issued and heard in health by teacher and student—the student (and sometimes the teacher, too) may resist it. For even when change is good and recognized as such by everyone involved in the process, the prospect of change often triggers a natural instinct in conservative human nature to run away.

Change requires the transformation, and even the death, of the old. What is new arises, Phoenix-like, from the ashes of what has outlived its usefulness. Teachers do well to keep this "species truth" in mind when picturing how, and how quickly, they wish their students to change. It is not easy to leave the comfort of one's small and sleepy village in order to cross a threshold that, however enticing, is also an enigma.

Having crossed the threshold—which is really an ongoing affair of ever more powerful forms of the student's engagement with the curriculum, teacher, classmates, and ultimately himself—the student enters the forest of adventure called the classroom. His guide, of course, is the teacher, who, although a fellow-traveler in search of existential refinement, functions primarily as a Wise Elder. Ideally, this archetypal role is filled by someone who has reflected often and seriously on herself in personal, professional, and political terms, for only such a teacher is sufficiently aware of both her gifts and limitations, her insights and biases, to be able to imbibe the archetypal nectar of her role in a way that enlivens her sensibilities and does not make her drunk with power. Such a teacher knows how to encourage the student to test out certain boundaries; and the wisdom to suggest to the venturing student which boundaries are best left uncrossed.

Naturally, the hero-student undergoes various tests in his journey. When the tests are authentic, they help a student see how much his grasp of something has evolved. They help him and his teacher begin to realistically assess his interests and potentials in various areas. These assessments should be multimodal, wide-ranging, and ongoing, however, or else the student will almost certainly wind up being pigeonholed with vital aspects of his existence neglected. No one is good at everything, but everyone should be given the chance to develop each aspect of his being as much as possible. Authentic assessment sees this as not only a pedagogical reality, but also an existential one—and builds upon it to form richly student-centered curricula.

In short, when assessment exists to help students cultivate each aspect of their multifaceted existence, it is serving holistic, integrative, and transformative purposes. It is heroic. When, on the other hand, testing is used simply as a way of getting students—through the use of obscene rewards and draconian punishments—to become compliant objects of irrelevant, unhealthy agendas imposed on them by some corporate entity or other, then it ceases to be authentic. It becomes an instrument of oppression. Assessment that furthers the student's heroic journey is deep. Testing that (through either seduction or shame) alienates the student from himself is toxic.

On the road of academic adventure, the student is not alone. He has his teacher and classmates by his side. Together, they make common cause in forming a community of inquiry and experimentation. But community need not mean conformity. A community of inquiry is one in which each individual explores and expands his uniqueness through encounter with multiple points of view. This being a process that can only occur in an atmosphere of civility, the student learns how to affirm, or at least tolerate, perspectives and practices that may not completely correspond to his own, or may not correspond at all. Nevertheless, he grows more able to see whatever value may genuinely inhere in those perspectives and practices. He becomes "civil" in the basic meaning of the word—willing and able to coexist with others in an enlightened democratic fashion. Students also begin to gain inroads into larger circles of discourse outside the classroom by learning how members of various professional communities think and communicate. In this sense, students become cognitive apprentices in those communities—an apprenticeship that may prove so rewarding for certain students that they become official members and, ultimately, cognitive masters in that community one day.

Above all else, heroic education is dedicated to the student's individuation—a lifelong process of bringing contrarieties into fruitful interaction, as in the creation and nurturance of the ego-Self axis. This axis provides the ego with higher standards by which to operate; at the same time, it allows the Self to incarnate and unfold in the world and for the world. But whatever the dichotomies involved in the individuation process—sensation and intuition, thinking and feeling, extroversion and introversion, the conscious and the unconscious, science and art—they all ultimately reflect the overarching cosmic dialectic between the archetypally masculine and feminine principles, the Great Father and the Great Mother, which, as one of the most ancient religious texts in the world, the *Tao Te Ching*, informs us, constitutes the essential dynamic of the universe. Educationally, this archetypal bifurcation manifests itself in the classroom in the Great Mother's desire to promote emotional health, intuitive inspiration, and poetic vision in her children; and in the Great Father's project of developing cognitive clarity, critical acumen, and pragmatic power in them.

When these two principles unite in a classroom, what emerges from this royal wedding of Rex and Regina is a balanced, authoritative pedagogy working in the service of the teacher's and students' individuation. This results in the Great Reward of the transcendent function, the Pearl of Great Price or the Sword Excalibur, which the teacher and students can now claim as their own because they have discovered it and learned how to use it together during their classroom journey.

This is the heroic vision of education. It honors teachers and students as free agents who, dedicated to discovering and developing the best in themselves and others, create change that is powerful and humane. For in the last analysis, the heroic journey is a lifelong educational process, and the village to which the hero is always returning, in order to reform and revitalize it, is nothing less than the global village—the world itself.

Bibliography

Abrams, M. H. 1973. *Natural supernaturalism: Tradition and revolution in Romantic literature*. New York: W. W. Norton.

Adams, M. 1996. *The multicultural imagination: "Race," color, and the unconscious*. London: Routledge.

Adler, M. J. 1982. *The Paideia proposal: An educational manifesto*. New York: Macmillan.

Aichhorn, A. 1925. *Wayward youth: A psychoanalytic study of delinquent children, illustrated by actual case histories*. New York: Viking Press.

Anderson, R., and P. Hopkins. 1991. *The feminine face of God: The unfolding of the sacred in women*. New York: Bantam Books.

Anthony, E. 1989. The psychoanalytic approach to learning theory (with more than a passing reference to Piaget). In K. Field, B. Cohler, and G. Wool (eds.), *Learning and education: Psychoanalytic perspectives* (pp. 99-126). Madison, CT: International Universities Press.

Anyon, J. 2001. Inner cities, affluent suburbs, and unequal educational opportunity. In J. Banks and C. Banks (eds.), *Multicultural education: Issues and perspectives* (pp. 85-102). New York: John Wiley and Sons.

Apple, M. 1990. *Ideology and curriculum*. London: Routledge.

Banks, J. and C. Banks (eds.). 2001. *Multicultural education: Issues and perspectives* (4th edition). New York: Wiley.

Barzun, J. 2000. *From dawn to decadence: 500 years of Western cultural life*. New York: HarperCollins.

Basch, M. 1989. The teacher, the transference, and development. In K. Field, B. Cohler, and G. Wool (eds.), *Learning and education: Psychoanalytic perspectives* (pp. 771-788). Madison, CT: International Universities Press.

Belenky, M., B. Clinchy, N. Goldberger, and J. Tarule. 1986. *Women's way of knowing*. New York: Basic Books.

Bernstein, B. 1971. *Class, codes, and control* (volume 1). London, Boston and Henley: Routledge & Keagan Paul.

Bernstein, B. 1996. *Pedagogy, symbolic control, and identity: Theory, research, critique*. London: Taylor and Francis.

Big Brother, Big Business. 2006. *A CNBC Special Report*. First aired November 9, 2006.

Blos, P. 1940. *The adolescent personality: A study of individual behavior for the Commission on Secondary School Curriculum*. New York: D. Appleton-Century.

Bourdieu, P. 1977. Cultural reproduction. In J. Karabel, and A. Halsey (eds.), *Power and ideology in education* (pp. 487-507). New York: Oxford Press.

Bowles, S., and H. Gintis. 1976. *Schooling in capitalist America*. New York: Basic Books.

Brophy, J. 1994. *Motivating students to learn*. Boston: McGraw-Hill.

Brown, J. S., A. Collins, and S. Duguid. 1989. Situated cognition and the culture of learning. *Educational Researcher, 18*(1), 32-42.

Bruner, J. 1960. *The process of education*. New York: Vintage.

Bruner, J. 1996. *The culture of education*. Cambridge, MA: Harvard University Press.

Buber, M. 1965. *I and thou*. New York: Vintage.

Bullough, R., Jr. 1989. *First-year teacher: A case study*. New York: Teachers College Press.

Bullough, R., Jr. 2001. *Uncertain lives: Children of hope, teachers of promise*. New York: Teachers College Press.

Burke, K. 1989. *On symbols and society*. Edited and with an introduction by J. Gusfield. Chicago: University of Chicago Press.

Campbell, J. 1949. *The hero with a thousand faces*. Princeton, NJ: Princeton University Press.

Castoriadis, C. 1994. Psychoanalysis and politics. In S. Shamdasani and M. Munchow (eds.), *Speculations after Freud: Psychoanalysis, philosophy, and culture* (pp. 1-12). London: Routledge.

Chinn, C., and W. Brewer. 1993. The role of anomalous data in knowledge acquisition: A theoretical framework and implications for science instruction. *Review of Educational Research, 63*(1), 1-49.

Chodorow, N. 1978. *The reproduction of mothering: Psychoanalysis and the sociology of gender*. Berkeley: University of California Press.

Cohler, B. 1989. Psychoanalysis and education: Motive, meaning, and self. In K. Field, B. Cohler, and G. Wool (eds.), *Learning and education: Psychoanalytic perspectives* (pp.11-84). Madison, CT: International Universities Press.

Conforti, M. 1999. *Field, form, and fate: Patterns in mind, nature, and psyche*. Woodstock, CT: Spring Publications.

Conger, J., and J. Galambos. 1997. *Adolescence and youth: Psychological development in a changing world*. New York: Longman.

Cook, B. (ed.). 2008. *Women writing nature: A feminist view*. Lanham, MD: Lexington Books.

Cozzarrelli, L., and M. Silin. 1989. The effects of narcissistic transferences on the teaching-learning process. In K. Field, B. Cohler, and G. Wool (eds.), *Learning and education: Psychoanalytic perspectives* (pp. 809-824). Madison, CT: International Universities Press.

Craig, R. 1994. The face we put on: Carl Jung for teachers. *The Clearing House, 67*(4), 189-191.

Cremin, L. 1964. *The transformation of the school: Progressivism in American education, 1876-1957*. New York: Vintage Press.

Cremin, L. 1988. *American education: The metropolitan experience*. New York: Harper and Row.

Crenshaw, K. 1995. *Critical race theory: The key writings that formed the movement*. New York: New Press.

Cudworth, E. 2005. *Developing ecofeminist theory: The complexity of difference*. New York: Palgrave Macmillan.

De Castillejo, I. 1973. *Knowing woman: A feminine psychology*. New York: Harper and Row.

Devine, D. 1995. Prejudice and out-group perception. In A. Tesser (ed.), *Advanced social psychology* (pp. 467-524). New York: McGraw-Hill.

Dewey, J. 1916. *Democracy and education*. New York: Macmillan.

Deyhle, D. 1986. Break dancing and breaking out: Anglos, Utes, and Navajos in a border reservation school. *Anthropology and Education Quarterly, 19*(4), 354-382.

Doctrine and Covenants of the Church of Jesus Christ of Latter-day Saints, The. Salt Lake City, Utah: The Church of Jesus Christ of Latter-day Saints.

Dole, J., and G. Sinatra. 1994. Social psychology research on beliefs and attitudes: Implications for research on learning from text. In R. Garner and P. Alexander (eds.), *Beliefs about texts and instruction with text* (pp. 245-264). Hillsdale, NJ: Lawrence Erlbaum Associates.

Dole, J., D. Niederhauser, and M. Hayes. 1991. The role of reading in conceptual change in science. Paper presented at the meeting of the American Educational Research Association. Chicago, April, 1991.

Dorn, C., S. Stanley, and F. R. Madeja. 2004. *Assessing expressive learning: A practical guide for teacher-directed, authentic assessment in K-12 visual arts education*. Mahwah, NJ: Lawrence Erlbaum Associates.

Eagle, M. 1993. *Recent developments in psychoanalysis: A critical evaluation*. Cambridge, MA: Harvard University Press.

Edinger, E. 1973. *Ego and archetype: Individuation and the religious function of the psyche*. Baltimore, MD: Penguin Press.

Eisner, E., and E. Vallance. 1985. *The educational imagination: On the design and evaluation of school programs*. New York: Macmillan.

Ekstein, R., and R. Motto. 1969. *From learning for love to love of learning: Essays on psychoanalysis and education*. New York: Brunner/Mazel.

Ellenberger, H. 1970. *The discovery of the unconscious: The history and evolution of dynamic psychiatry*. New York: Basic Books.

Elson, M. 1989. The teacher as learner, the learner as teacher. In K. Field, B. Cohler, and G. Wool (eds.), *Learning and education: Psychoanalytic perspectives* (pp. 789-808). Madison, CT: International Universities Press.

Fairbairn, W. R. D. 1992. *Psychoanalytic studies of the personality*. London: Routledge.

Fay, B. 2000. *Contemporary philosophy of social science: A multicultural approach*. Oxford: Blackwell.

Ferdman, B. M. 1990. Literacy and cultural identity. *Harvard Educational Review, 60*(2), 181-204.

Field, K. 1989. Some reflections on the teacher-student dialogue: A psychoanalytic perspective. In K. Field, B. Cohler, and G. Wool (eds.), *Learning and education: Psychoanalytic perspectives* (pp. 851-926). Madison, CT: International Universities Press.

Forbes, S. 2003. *Holistic education: An analysis of its nature and ideas*. Brandon, VT: Foundation for Educational Renewal Press.

Foucault, M. 1975. *The birth of the clinic*. New York: Vintage Books.

Freire, P. 1970. *The pedagogy of the oppressed*. New York: Seabury Press.

Freire, P. 2001. *Pedagogy and freedom: Ethics, democracy, and civic courage*. Lanham, MD: Rowman & Littlefield.

Freud, A. 1930. *Introduction to psychoanalysis: Lectures for child analysts and teachers, 1922-1935*. New York: International Universities Press.

Freud, S. 1957 [1914]. On narcissism: An introduction. In J. Rickman (ed.), *A general selection from the works of Sigmund Freud* (pp. 104-123). New York: Doubleday.

Freud, S. 1957 [1923]. The ego and the id. In J. Rickman (ed.), *A general selection from the works of Sigmund Freud* (pp. 210-235). New York: Doubleday.

Freud, S. 1970 [1915-1917]. *A general introduction to psycho-analysis*. Translated by J. Riviere. New York: Simon and Schuster.

Frey-Rohn, L. 1974. *From Freud to Jung: A comparative study of the psychology of the unconscious*. New York: G. P. Putnam's Sons.

Friedman, T. 2000. *The Lexus and the olive tree: Understanding globalization*. New York: Anchor Books.

Garcia, E. 2001. *Hispanic education in the United States: Raices y aulas*. Landham, MD: Rowman & Littlefield.

Gardner, H. 1983. *Frames of mind*. New York: Basic Books.

Garner, R. 1990. Do readers change their minds while reading persuasive text? An unpublished paper. Washington State University, Vancouver.

Gellert, M. 2001. *The fate of America: An inquiry into national character*. Washington, DC: Brassey's.

Giddens, A. 1990. *The consequences of modernity*. Stanford, CA: Stanford University Press.

Giddens, A. 2002. *Runaway world: How globalization is reshaping our lives*. London: Profile.

Gilligan, C. 1982. *In a different voice: Psychological theory and women's development*. Cambridge, MA: Harvard University Press.

Giroux, H. 1983. Theories of reproduction and resistance in the new sociology of education: A critical analysis. *Harvard Educational Review*, *53*(3), 257-293.

Giroux, H., and K. Myrciades (eds.). 2001. *Beyond the corporate university: Culture and pedagogy in the new millennium*. Lanham, MD: Rowman & Littlefield.

Goldbrunner, J. 1965. *Individuation: A study of the depth psychology of Carl Gustav Jung*. Notre Dame, IN: University of Notre Dame Press.

Gonzalez, N. 2001. *I am my language: Discourses of women and children in the borderlands*. Tucson: University of Arizona Press.

Gray, R. 1996. *Archetypal explorations: An integrative approach to human behavior*. London: Routledge.

Greene, M. 1975. *Education, freedom, and possibility*. New York: Teachers College Press.

Greenson, R. 1990. The working alliance and the transference neurosis. In A. Esman (ed.), *Essential papers on transference* (pp. 150-171). New York: University Press.

Grossman, B. 1975. Freud and the classroom. In T. Roberts (ed.), *Four psychologies applied to education: Freudian, behavioral, humanistic, transpersonal* (pp. 63-69). Cambridge, MA: Schenkman.

Halliday, M. 1975. *Learning how to mean*. London: Edward Arnold.

Harding, M. E. 1973. *Psychic energy: Its source and its transformation*. Princeton, NJ: Bollingen Press.

Heath, S. 1983. *Ways with words: Language, life, and work in communities and classrooms*. Cambridge, England: Cambridge University Press.

Henderson, J. 1967. *Thresholds of initiation*. Middletown, CT: Wesleyan University Press.

Hoffer, E. 1966. *The true believer: Thoughts on the nature of mass movements*. New York: Harper and Row.

Huebner, D. 1999. *The lure of the transcendent: Collected essays by Dwayne E. Huebner*. Mahwah, NJ: Lawrence Erlbaum Associates.

Jacobi, J. 1974. *Complex/archetype/symbol in the psychology of C. G. Jung*. Princeton, NJ: Princeton University Press.

Janesick, V. 2006. *Authentic assessment primer*. New York: Peter Lang.

Jones, G. M., B. D. Jones, and T. Hargrove. 2003. *The unintended consequences of high-stakes testing*. Lanham, MD: Rowman & Littlefield.

Jones, R. 1968. *Fantasy and feeling in education*. New York: New York University Press.

Joseph, P., and G. Burnaford. 1994. *Images of schoolteachers in twentieth-century America: Paragons, polarities, complexities*. New York: St. Martin's Press.

Jung, C. G. 1921. *Psychological types*. Translated by R. F. C. Hull. (Volume 6 in the *Collected works*). Princeton, NJ: Princeton University Press.

Jung, C. G. 1953. *Two essays on analytical psychology*. Translated by R. F. C. Hull. (Volume 7 in the *Collected works*). Princeton, NJ: Princeton University Press.

Jung, C. G. 1954. *The practice of psychotherapy: Essays on the psychology of the transference and other subjects*. Translated by R. F. C. Hull. (Volume 16 in the *Collected works*). Princeton, NJ: Princeton University Press.

Jung, C. G. 1956. *Symbols of transformation: Analysis of the prelude to a case of schizophrenia*. Translated by R. F. C. Hull. (Volume 5 in the *Collected works*). Princeton, NJ: Princeton University Press.

Jung, C. G. 1958. *Psychology and religion: West and East*. Translated by R. F. C. Hull. (Volume 11 in the *Collected works*). Princeton, NJ: Princeton University Press.

Jung, C. G. 1960. *The structure and dynamics of the psyche*. Translated by R. F. C. Hull. (Volume 8 in the *Collected works*). Princeton, NJ: Princeton University Press.

Jung, C. G. 1963. *Mysterium coniuncionis*. Translated by R. F. C. Hull. (Volume 14 in the *Collected works*). Princeton, NJ: Princeton University Press.

Jung, C. G. 1966. *The spirit in man, art, and literature*. Translated by R. F. C. Hull. (Volume 15 in the *Collected works*). Princeton, NJ: Princeton University Press.

Jung, C. G. 1968a. The archetypes and the collective unconscious. Translated by R. F. C. Hull. (Volume 9.1 in the Collected works). Princeton, NJ: Princeton University Press.

Jung, C. G. 1968b. *Aion: Researches into the phenomenology of the self*. Translated by R. F. C. Hull. (Volume 9.2 in the *Collected works*). Princeton, NJ: Princeton University Press.

Jung, C. G. 1968c. *Alchemical studies*. Translated by R. F. C. Hull. (Volume 13 in the *Collected works*). Princeton, NJ: Princeton University Press.

Jung, C. G. 1977. *The symbolic life: Miscellaneous writings*. Translated by G. Adler and R. F. C. Hull. (Volume 18 in the *Collected works*). Princeton, NJ: Princeton University Press.

Jung, C. G., and A. Jaffé. 1965. *Memories, dreams, reflections*. New York: Vintage.

Jung, E., and M.-L. Von Franz. 1986. *The Grail legend*. London: Coventure.

Kant, I. 2007. *Critique of pure reason*. New York: Palgrave Macmillan.

Kantor, H. 1988. *Learning to earn: School, work, and vocational reform in California, 1889-1930*. Madison: University of Wisconsin Press.

Kaulback, B. 1989. Styles of learning among Native children: A review of the research. In B. Shade (ed.), *Culture, style, and the educative process* (pp. 137-149). Springfield, IL: Charles C Thomas.

Keefe, J., and J. Jenkins. 2008. *Personalized instruction: The key to student achievement*. Lanham, MD: Rowman & Littlefield.

Kirman, W. 1977. *Modern psychoanalysis in the schools*. Dubuque, IA: Kendall/Hunt.

Klinenberg, E. 2007. *Fighting for air: The battle to control America's media*. New York: Metropolitan Books.

Kohut, H. 1978. *The search for self: Selected writings of Heinz Kohut: 1950-1978*. Edited by P. Ornstein. Madison, CT: International Universities Press.

Kozol, J. 1991. *Savage inequalities: Children in American schools*. New York: Harper.

Kubie, L. 1967. The forgotten man of education. In R. Jones (ed.), *Contemporary educational psychology: Selected readings* (pp. 61-71). New York: Harper and Row.

Kuhn, T. 1970. *The structure of scientific revolutions*. Chicago: University of Chicago Press.

Lauter, E., and C. Rupprecht. 1985. *Feminist archetypal theory: Interdisciplinary re-visions of Jungian thought*. Knoxville: The University of Tennessee Press.

Lévi-Strauss, C. 1987. *Anthropology and myth: Lectures, 1951-1982*. Translated by R. Willis. New York: Blackwell.

Lipman, M. 1988. *Philosophy goes to school*. Philadelphia: Temple University Press.

Lortie, D. 1975. *Schoolteacher: A sociological study*. Chicago: University of Chicago Press.

MacLeod, J. 1987. *Ain't no makin' it: Leveled aspirations in a low-income neighborhood*. Boulder, CO: Westview Press.

Marx, K. 1978. *The Marx-Engels reader*. Edited by R. Tucker. New York: W. W. Norton.

Maslow, A. 1968. *Toward a psychology of being* (2nd edition). Princeton, NJ: D. Van Nostrand.

Mattoon, M. A. 1981. *Jungian psychology in perspective*. New York: Free Press.

May, R., and I. Yalom. 1995. Existential psychotherapy. In R. Corsini and D. Wedding (eds.), *Current psychotherapies* (pp. 262-292). Itasca, IL: F. E. Peacock.

Mayes, C. 1998. The use of contemplative practices in teacher education. *Encounter: Education for Meaning and Social Justice, 11*(3), 17-31.

Mayes, C. 1999. Reflecting on the archetypes of teaching. *Teaching Education, 10*(2), 3-16.

Mayes, C. 2001. Deepening our reflectivity. *The Teacher Educator, 36*(4), 248-264.

Mayes, C. 2002a. The teacher as an archetype of spirit. *Journal of Curriculum Studies, 34*(6), 699-718.

Mayes, C. 2002b. Personal and archetypal aspects of transference and counter-transference in the classroom. *Encounter: Education for Meaning and Social Justice, 15*(2), 34-49.

Mayes, C. 2003a. *Seven curricular landscapes: An approach to the holistic curriculum*. Lanham, MD: University Press of America.

Mayes, C. 2003b. Alchemy and the teacher. *The Teacher Education Quarterly, 30*(3), 81-98.

Mayes, C. 2004. *Teaching mysteries: Foundations of spiritual pedagogy*. Lanham, MD: University Press of America.

Mayes, C. 2005. *Jung and education: Elements of an archetypal pedagogy*. Lanham, MD: Rowman & Littlefield.

Mayes, C. 2007. *Inside education: Depth psychology in teaching and learning*. Madison, WI: Atwood Publishing.

Mayes, C., and P. Blackwell Mayes. 2002. Spiritual reflectivity among Mormon teachers and administrators in the public schools. *International Journal of Leadership in Education, 5*(2), 129–148.

Mayes, C., and P. Blackwell Mayes. 2005. Jung, Mormonism, and the dialectics of exaltation. *Psychological Perspectives: A Semiannual Journal of Jungian Thought* (C.G. Institute of Los Angeles), *48*, 84–107

Mayes, C., R. Maile Cutri, C. Rogers, and F. Montero. 2007. *Understanding the whole student: Holistic multicultural education*. Lanham, MD: Rowman & Littlefield.

Mayes, C. 2009. The psychoanalytic view of teaching and learning: 1922-2002. *Journal of Curriculum Studies,* 41(4), 539-567.

McChesney, R. W. 2004. *The problem of the media: U.S. communication politics in the 21st century*. New York: Monthly Review Press.

Meissner, W. 1984. *Psychoanalysis and religious experience*. New Haven: Yale University Press.

Mezeske, R., and B. Mezeske. 2007. *Beyond tests and quizzes: Creative assessments in the college classroom*. San Francisco: Jossey-Bass.

Miller, J. 1988. *The holistic curriculum*. Toronto: The Ontario Institute for Studies in Education.

Miller, J. 2004. *The transcendent function : Jung's model of psychological growth through dialogue with the unconscious*. Albany: State University of New York Press.

National Commission on Excellence in Education. 1983. *A nation at risk: The imperative for educational reform* (p. 5). Washington, DC: United States Government Printing Office.

Neumann, E. 1954. *The origins and history of consciousness* (volume 1). Translated by R. F. C. Hull. New York: Harper Brothers.

Neumann, E. 1985. *Anatomy of the psyche: Alchemical symbolism in psychotherapy*. New York: Lightning Source.

New English Bible (NEB). 2001. Oxford, England: Oxford University Press.

Nielsen, D. 2006. *Beloved bridegroom*. Provo, UT: Onyx Press.

Nieto, S. 2000. *Affirming diversity: The sociopolitical context of multicultural education*. New York: Addison, Wesley, Longman.

No Child Left Behind Act of 2002, The. (Pub.L. 107-110, 115 Stat. 1425.)

Noddings, N. 1999. Stories and conversations in schools. In J. Kane (ed.), *Education, information, and transformation: Essays on learning and thinking* (pp. 319–336). Columbus, OH: Merrill.

Oakes, J. 2000. The distribution of knowledge. In R. Arum and I. Beattie (eds.), *The structure of schooling: Readings in the sociology of education*. Mountain View, CA: Mayfield.

Odajnyk, V. 1976. *Jung and politics: The political and social ideas of C. G. Jung*. New York: Harper and Row.

Ogbu, J. 1987. Variability in minority school performance: A problem in search of an explanation. *Anthropology and Education Quarterly, 18*, 312-334.

Ornstein, A., and F. Hunkins. 1988. *Curriculum: Foundations, principles, and issues*. Boston: Allyn and Bacon.

Pagels, E. 1988. *Adam, Eve, and the Serpent*. New York: Random House.

Palmer, M. 1995. *Freud and Jung on religion*. New York: Routledge.

Pauson, M. 1988. *Jung the philosopher: Essays in Jungian thought*. New York: Peter Lang.

Pepper, F. 1989. Social and cultural effects on Indian Learning style. In B. Shade (ed.), *Culture, style, and the educative process* (pp. 137-149). Springfield, IL: Charles C Thomas.

Pfister, O. 1922. *Psycho-analysis in the service of education, being an introduction to psycho-analysis*. London: Henry Kimpton.

Pintrich, P., R. Marx, and R. Boyle. 1993. Beyond cold conceptual change: The role of motivational beliefs and classroom contextual factors in the process of conceptual change. *Review of Educational Research*, *63*, 167-199.

Posner, G. J., K. A. Strike, P. W. Hewson, and W. A. Gertzog. 1982. Accomodation of a scientific conception: Toward a theory of conceptual change. *Science Education*, *67*(4), 498-508.

Postman, N., and C. Weingartner. 1969. *Teaching as a subversive activity*. New York: Delacorte Press.

Redl, F., and W. Wattenberg. 1951. *Mental hygiene in teaching*. New York: Harcourt, Brace.

Resnick, L. 1987. The 1987 presidential address: Learning in school and out. *Educational Researcher*, *16*(9), 13-20.

Richards, A. L. 2007. Public education in the Third Reich. A paper delivered at Brigham Young University, Provo, Utah, May 15, 2007.

Rizzuto, A-M. 1979. *The birth of the living God: A psychoanalytic study*. Chicago: University of Chicago Press.

Robinson, J. M. (ed.). 1990. *The Nag Hammadi library: The definitive new translation of the Gnostic scriptures, complete in one volume* (rev. edition). New York: HarperCollins.

Rogoff, B. 2003. *The cultural nature of human development*. New York: Oxford University Press.

Rorty, R. 1981. *Philosophy and the mirror of nature*. Princeton, NJ: Princeton University Press.

Rummelhart, D. 1980. Schemata: The building blocks of cognition. In R. Spiro, B. Bruce, and W. Brewer (eds.), *Theoretical issues in reading comprehension* (pp. 125-167). Hillside, NJ: Lawrence Erlbaum Associates.

Sadker, M., and D. Sadker. 2004. *Failing at fairness: How America's schools cheat girls*. New York: Charles Scribner's Sons.

Salzberger-Wittenberg, I. 1989. *The emotional experience of learning and teaching*. London: Routledge and Kegan Paul.

Samuels, A. 1997. *Jung and the post-Jungians*. London: Routledge.

Sarason, S. 1999. *Teaching as a performing art*. New York: Teachers College Press.

Sartre, J. P. 1956. *Being and nothingness: An essay on phenomenological ontology*. New York: Philosophical Library.

Schafer, R. 1980. Narration in the psychoanalytic dialogue. *Critical Inquiry*, 7(1), 29-54.

Schön, D. 1987. *Educating the reflective practitioner*. San Francisco: Jossey-Bass.

Scott, P. D. 2003. *Drugs, oil, and war: The United States in Colombia, Afghanistan, and Indochina*. Lanham, MD: Rowman & Littlefield.

Scott, P. D. 2007. *The road to 9/11: Wealth, empire, and the future of America*. Berkeley: University of California Press.

Serow, R., D. Eaker, and J. Ciechalski. 1992. Calling, service, and legitimacy: Professional orientations and career commitment among prospective teachers. *Journal of Research and Development in Education, 25*(3): 136-141.

Shalem, Y., and D. Bensusan. 1999. Why can't we stop believing? In S. Appel (ed.), *Psychoanalysis and pedagogy* (pp. 27-44). London: Bergin and Garvey.

Shaker, P. 1982. The application of Jung's analytical psychology to education. *Journal of Curriculum Studies, 14*(3), 241-250.

Singer, J. 1988. Foreword. In D. Feinstein, and S. Krippner (eds.), *Personal mythology: Using rituals, dreams, and imagination to discover your inner story*. Los Angeles: Jeremy P. Tarcher.

Skinner, B. F. 1956. *The technology of teaching*. New York: Appleton-Century-Croft.

Spiegelman, J., and V. Mansfeld. 1996. On the physics and psychology of the transference as an interactive field. In J. Spiegelman (ed.), *Psychotherapy as a mutual process* (pp. 183-206). Tempe, AZ: New Falcon Publications.

Spindler, G. and L. Spindler. 1992. Cultural process and ethnography: An anthropological perspective. In M. LeCompte, W. Millroy, and J. Preissle (eds.), *The handbook of qualitative research in education* (pp. 52-92). London: Academic Press.

Spring, J. 1976. *The sorting machine: National educational policy since 1945*. New York: David McKay.

Stein, M. 1995. Power, shamanism, and maieutics in the countertransference. In N. Schwartz-Salant and M. Stein (eds.), *Transference/countertransference* (pp. 67-88). Wilmette, IL: Chiron Publications.

Stokes, D. 1997. Called to teach: Exploring the worldview of called prospective teachers during their preservice teacher education experience. An unpublished dissertation. Salt Lake City: University of Utah.

Tetreault, M. K. 2001. Gender bias: From colonial America to today's classrooms. In J. Banks and C. Banks (eds.), *Multicultural education: Issues and perspectives* (4th edition, pp. 125-151). New York: Wiley.

Tharp, R. G. 1989. Psychocultural variables and constants: Effects on teaching and learning in schools. *American Psychologist, 44*, 349-359.

Tillich, P. 1952. *The courage to be*. New Haven, CT: Yale University Press.

Trostli, R. 1991. Educating as an art: The Waldorf approach. In R. Miller (ed.), *New directions in education: Selections from* Holistic Education Review (pp. 338-353). Brandon, VT: Holistic Education Press.

Tyack, D. 1974. *The one best system: A history of American urban education*. Cambridge, MA: Harvard University Press.

Ulanov, A. 1999. *Religion and the spiritual in Carl Jung*. New York: Paulist Press.

Valli, L. 1990. Moral approaches to reflective practice. In R. Clift, W. Houston, and M. Pugach (eds.), *Encouraging reflective practice in education: An analysis of issues and programs* (pp. 39-56). New York: Teachers College Press.

Valli, L. 1993. Reflective teacher education programs: An analysis of case studies. In J. Calderhead and P. Gates (eds.), *Conceptualizing reflection in teacher development* (pp.11-21). Washington, DC: Falmer Press.

Vivas, E. and M. Krieger (eds.). 1953. *The problems of aesthetics*. New York: Reinhart.

von Franz, M.-L. 1974. *Number and time: Reflections leading toward a unification of depth psychology and physics*. Evanston, IL: Northwestern University Press.

Vosniadou, S., and W. Brewer. 1987. Theories of knowledge restructuring in development. *Review of Educational Research*, 57, 51-67.

Vygotsky, L. 1986. *Mind in society: The development of psychological functions*. Cambridge, MA: Harvard University Press.

Wade, J. 1996. *Changes of mind: A holonomic theory of the evolution of consciousness*. Albany: State University of New York Press.

Watts, A. 1968. *The wisdom of insecurity: A message for an age of anxiety*. New York: Vintage.

Wax, M., R. Wax, and R. Dumont, Jr. 1964. *Formal education in an American Indian community: Peer society and the failure of minority education*. Prospect Heights, IL: Waveland Press.

Whitehead, A. N. 1967. *The aims of education, and other essays.* New York: Free Press.

Wilber, K. 2000. *Integral psychology*. Boston: Shambhala.

Winnicott, D. W. 1988 [1969]. *The mother-infant experience of mutuality*. In C. Winnicott, R. Shepherd, and M. Davis (eds.), *Psychoanalytic explorations* (pp. 251-260). Cambridge, MA: Harvard University Press.

Winnicott, D. W., R. Shepherd, and M. Davis (eds.). 1988. *Psychoanalytic explorations*. Cambridge, MA: Harvard University Press.

Winnicott, D. W., 1992. In C. Winnicott, R. Shepherd, and M. Davis (eds.), *Psychoanalytic explorations*. Cambridge, MA: Harvard University Press.

Wolf, E. 1989. The psychoanalytic self-psychologist looks at learning. In K. Field, B. Cohler, and G. Wool (eds.). *Learning and education: Psychoanalytic perspectives* (pp. 377-394). Madison, CT: International Universities Press.

Woodman, M. 1995. Transference and countertransference in analysis dealing with eating disorders. In N. Schwartz-Salant and M. Stein (eds.), *Transference/countertransference* (pp. 53-66). Wilmette, IL: Chiron Publications.

Wool, G. 1989. Relational aspects of learning: The learning alliance. In K. Field, B. Cohler, and G. Wool (eds.), *Learning and education: Psychoanalytic perspectives* (pp. 747-770). Madison, CT: International Universities Press.

Wertsch, J. 1985. *Vygotsky and the social formation of mind.* Cambridge, MA: Harvard University Press.

Zinn, H. 1990. *A people's history of the United States*. New York: Harper Perennial.

Index

F

G

H

I

J

K

L

M

N

O

P

V

W

Z

About the Author

Clifford Mayes is a professor of education at Brigham Young University in the Department of Educational Leadership and Foundations. He holds a doctorate from the University of Utah in The Cultural Foundations of Education and a doctorate from Southern California University for Professional Studies in Educational Psychology. Cliff grew up in a highly multicultural setting with a population comprised equally of Native Americans, Hispanic Americans, African Americans, and Caucasian Americans in the outskirts of Tucson, Arizona, in the 1950s and 1960s. He taught at universities in Panama and Japan throughout the 1980s. He is a recipient of the BYU Student Association Teacher-of-the-Year Award in Brigham Young University's McKay School of Education. His research centers around the deep psychological and cultural dimensions of teaching and learning.